To Gen.

I hope you *enjoy your journey*

Warmly,

Jim

SEARCHING FOR ROBERT
FINDING ANDREW

The Reunion Of Mother And Son

JILL L. O'DONNELL

Copyright © 2014 by Jill L. O'Donnell
First Edition – 2014

ISBN
978-1-4602-4768-6 (Hardcover)
978-1-4602-4769-3 (Paperback)
978-1-4602-4770-9 (eBook)

Produced by:

FriesenPress
Suite 300 – 852 Fort Street
Victoria, BC, Canada V8W 1H8

www.friesenpress.com

Distributed to the trade by The Ingram Book Company

Table of Contents

This book is dedicated to the memory of my mother, Doris Muretta Neufeld. Like me, she always hoped I would find my son, the grandson she dearly wanted to know.

Legacy of an Adopted Child

Once there were two women who never knew each other.
One you do not remember, the other you call Mother.
Two different lives shaped to make you one.
One became your guiding star, the other became your sun.
The first one gave you life, the second one taught you to live it.
The first one gave you a need for love, the
second one was there to give it.
One gave you a nationality, the other gave you a name.
One gave you a talent, the other gave you aim.
One gave you emotions, the other calmed your fears.
One saw your first sweet smile, the other dried your tears.
One sought for you a home she could not provide.
The other prayed for a child and her hope was not denied.
And now you ask me through your tears,
The age-old questions unanswered through the years,
Heredity or environment—which are you a product of?
Neither, my darling, neither—
Just two different kinds of love.

Author unknown

ACKNOWLEDGMENTS

A special thanks to my husband Leo whose encouragement and faith in me to write this memoir has never faltered.

Many thanks to Karen Amardeil, my instructor in Memoir Writing, for her constant encouragement to " keep on writing", to my fellow classmates and my Memoir Writing group, Nancy-Anne Purre, Elaine Graham, Pam Turner and Cory Lemos whose backing and support kept me on course.

I appreciate all the friendship and advice from colleagues, friends and family.

Special thanks to Jody Hagel my Account Manager the staff at FriesenPress for all their help in getting this book published.

Most of all my heart-felt thanks to Andrew for it is in finding him that has given me the incentive and purpose for sharing my story with others.

REFLECTIONS

Oh my God. I am going to be late. I don't want to make him wait.

My heart is pounding so hard I can hear it. *I hope I look ok.*

I glance at my face in the rear-view mirror.

Hair in place. Yep. Lipstick on. Yep.

Hurrying away from my car, I hear a "click" confirming the doors are locked. In my haste I stumble on the car park's slippery steps.

I should have worn winter boots.

Outside, I can barely see through the continuous thick veil of snow. It is ten to six.

Only ten minutes left.

Despite the cold winter night, I can feel the beads of perspiration making my blouse stick to my back.

Why didn't I give myself more time to get here?

Bitter wind sends a shiver through my entire body as it slaps my face and plasters fat snowflakes onto my coat. In my vanity, I've neglected to wear a hat and scarf. It is January 2010, and Toronto weather in January can never be counted on. Tonight is no exception.

I pull up the collar of my coat to protect my face and make a mad dash across York Street, dodging the heavy rush-hour traffic. I manage to get to the other side unscathed. Touching my large, bulging brown leather handbag, I hope I have packed all the items I wanted to bring with me.

Too late to worry about that now!

Pulling on that exterior door to the west lobby of the Royal York on a windy winter night is like trying to hold an umbrella from turning inside out. It takes all my strength to manoeuvre my body through the opening.

I grasp the brass hand railing as I run down the marble steps, fearful that, despite my three-year new knees, I'll tumble. I feel like a little kid on Christmas morning, anxious to open my presents, not knowing what is inside, yet fearful I may not like the contents.

Reaching the elevators, I glance at my watch; it is already six o'clock. I so desperately wanted to be here first to have time to relax and unwind.

No chance of that now.

Ten elevators, but not one there for me. Memories from that fated 1962 with John start flooding my mind.

Where is the darned elevator? I won't be there first.

My mouth goes dry. Finally an elevator arrives. I shrug off my coat and try to regain my composure. Thank goodness I am alone in the elevator, because I'm muttering, "Hurry up. Hurry up!"

Seconds seem like hours until the doors open. Rushing across the lobby to the restaurant, l hope to appear in control, with a certain *je ne sais quoi.*

"Bonsoir Madame. Do you have a reservation?"

TELLING JOHN

This can't happen to me, I thought. *It only happens to others. Other girls, but not me.*

Finding myself pregnant in February 1962 was a disgrace, not only to me, but to family and friends, should they find out. I was in the middle of a post-graduate course in Public Health Nursing at the University of Toronto.

Do I tell John or do I break off with him and go it on my own?

It was a going to be a tough decision.

Five months earlier

The party was in full swing by the time my friend Donna and I arrived at the Frat House on St. George Street.

"You look great. I love the perm," said Donna as we reached the front door. "You're smart—I should have worn my flats, too. They're better for dancing." The lights were turned down so low that we could barely make out the couples dancing in the living room to the soft sounds of Ray Coniff. Those who weren't dancing were seated on worn-out couches and chairs around the periphery of the room, and the combination of beer and cigarette smoke made it smell like the local pub. The side tables were laden with overflowing ashtrays and empty glasses.

Poking my head into the living room area to see if anybody I knew was there, I heard, "Hi Jill, how ya doin'?"

It was Tommy, a member at the Frat. I waved a hello.

"Great! Say hi to Donna," I said.

Tommy waved at Donna.

We made our way past several people with drinks in hand, standing in the hallway. A rather tall, friendly fellow in a University of Toronto navy bomber jacket gave us a big smile.

"Just keep going, ladies," he said, pointing towards the kitchen at the back of the house. "That's where you can find some libation."

Entering the kitchen, I was instantly drawn to a pleasant-looking young man; he was in animated conversation with another fellow at the far end of the room. There was something about him I found appealing. He was of medium height, and had brown hair and hazel eyes. I liked the way his eyes crinkled when he laughed. I blushed when he looked at me with a warm smile and a nod of his head. I knew I had his attention. He was smartly-dressed in a navy blue suit, white shirt, and navy and white striped tie. Since he wasn't in casual attire like most of the fellows there, I assumed he'd come directly from work.

The next thing I knew, he was taking me all in as he strode towards me with an outstretched hand.

For sure he is interested, I thought. I extended my hand to him.

"Hi, I'm John," he said with a generous smile. He made me feel completely at ease. I liked that he didn't tower over me. His very presence warmed my heart.

"Hi to you, too. I'm Jill," I said as I twirled my hair around a finger.

"Can I get you a drink?" he asked, heading for a table laden with food and beverages. "If you want white wine or beer, I'm told it's in the fridge

Like a moth drawn to a flame, I followed him. "I think I'll have a gin and tonic," I said, picking up a glass for him to fill.

Standing beside him, my heart skipped a beat. Suddenly I felt my cheeks heating up. *I can't remember the last time any fellow made me blush.*

Handing me my gin and tonic, he said, "Let's dance!"

Drinks in hand, we headed to the front room. The "In Crowd" by the Ramsay Lewis Trio was being played on the phonograph sitting on top of the piano. Putting our drinks down on a side table, John pulled me close. I liked the fact that we fit so well together.

"You're quite a good dancer," I commented as John swung me around the room.

"Thanks. You follow well!"

Most university guys could barely shuffle around the floor. Suddenly we were laughing and giggling as we did the twist to a Chubby Checker record.

It was clear that John had an excellent ability to change dancing style easily. Slow dancing to the Glenn Miller orchestra allowed me to enjoy the delicate spices of his after-shave. In fact, I felt light-headed.

"What brings you here?" John whispered in my ear as his lips brushed my cheek.

"I've been coming here for a couple of years now. It's a perfect place to meet new people, like you, for instance." I soon learned that John was from Hamilton and had recently secured a position with a Trust Company in Toronto. When I commented on his interesting accent, he told me he was Dutch.

We spent the rest of the evening together, and I was thrilled to bits when John asked to take me home. That early September meeting was the beginning of a whirlwind courtship. I was immediately smitten, as was he. What appealed to me most was John's solid approach to life, his intellectual pursuits, and his enjoyment of classical music. Neither of us wasted any time introducing our parents to the fact we were a pair. Before Christmas, I had the diamond to prove it.

By February, I had missed two periods and was certain I was pregnant. I lived in a large two-bedroom apartment building on Wellesley Street with three nursing classmates and an x-ray technician. To save money, I walked to both university and work.

Trying to focus on what I should do about my situation absorbed a huge portion of my waking hours. Finally one evening, while on relief duty at Women's College Hospital, I plucked up the courage to speak to Dr. Papsin, a Resident in Obstetrics and Gynaecology.

"Would you have time to go for coffee with me before I give out the evening medications?" I asked.

"Sure. Meet you in the cafeteria at nine o'clock."

After sharing my story with him over coffee, Dr. Papsin asked, "How far along do you think you are?"

"My last period was in December. I have morning nausea and my breasts have started to swell. They're pretty sore, too."

Without being judgmental, Dr. Papsin queried, "What do you want to do now?"

In 1962, birth control was not an open topic of discussion, whether with one's own doctor or peer group. Abortions were illegal. I had friends who were lucky enough to abort after taking certain medications. That choice did not appeal to me. It was too risky. Contraception was very new and it was not easy getting access to it. I knew I was cornered and that frightened me a lot. John and I had taken a chance having unprotected sex. We played Russian roulette and lost.

Having had two months to ruminate on being pregnant, my final decision was to have the baby and give it up for adoption. I definitely did not want to be forced into marriage. A couple of my nursing classmates had married because they were pregnant. Neither John nor I were established enough in our careers to take on marriage and a child. I was scared. I didn't dare talk about it with my roommates for fear of rejection. Most of all, I had to get through this post-graduate course in public health nursing. It wouldn't end until April, and then I still had to do a month of fieldwork. I couldn't stop wondering what my parents would think if they learned their only daughter was pregnant, and I didn't want to know. I was unwilling to share my knowledge with anyone other than John.

I hope I can keep this a secret, I thought. *Now I need to formulate a plan before telling John.*

"Once you have firmer plans," Dr. Papsin assured me, "I will help you as much as I can."

A few days later, I was getting ready for bed when one of my roommates called me to the phone.

"It's for you," she said, handing me the receiver. "It's John." I felt the hair on the back of my neck stand up. In fact, I felt slightly squeamish.

"Hi, John, how nice to hear from you," I said, trying to sound upbeat.

"I've managed to get tickets for the symphony Thursday night," he said. With hope and enthusiasm in his voice, he asked, "Can you go?"

"Absolutely. I'm working tomorrow night, so I'll be off on Thursday." *Wow, maybe I will have a chance to tell John when I see him. I certainly can't talk about it here where everyone can hear my conversation.*

"Super. I'll pick you up at seven o'clock," John replied before we went onto other topics. Just as he was ready to hang up, he said, "We can take our time and walk to Massey Hall."

A plan began to percolate in my mind. If possible, I would invite John up for coffee after the symphony and devise a way to tell him. Thursday was two days away. I rehearsed many different opening lines without deciding on any of them. They all felt lame. I hoped that when I was alone with John I would have the conviction to tell him.

Resident conductor Walter Susskind conducted the all-Bach program. Our seats were "in the Gods", as that is all John could afford. Throughout the program, John held my hand, often rubbing his hand softly over the back of mine as he leaned in closer. Being with him gave me a warm, all-over glow.

Leaving Massey Hall, we laughed as we fought the crowds down the long descent of several sets of stairs. Halfway down, I commented, "Are you game to walk back to my place?" I really needed time to shore up courage before telling him.

We were warmly dressed in our winter coats, hats, and gloves. John had on his trademark fedora and his toe rubbers; I was in my winter boots. Struggling to put his overcoat on over his navy blue suit, he said, "That's fine by me."

Heading out to the sidewalk, John pulled me close to him. "Wasn't that a marvellous performance?" he enthused as the leaned over to kiss me.

"It sure was!"

"Be careful, it's slippery," John commented, taking firm hold of my arm as we made our way through the crunchy snow and icy sidewalks. Ploughed snow was piled high on both sides of the road.

"Have you time to come up for a coffee?" I asked, trying to sound cheerful.

"Sure, it's not that late."

I knew some of my roommates were at work, and the others would be sleeping, so John and I would be alone. He was in such a good mood that I decided this would be the right time to share my news with him.

Sitting on our worn-out Goodwill-chic burgundy sofa, with the coffee cups and cookies on the makeshift coffee table in front us, John and I listened to the smoky, sultry seductive sounds of Nancy Wilson playing quietly in the background. We were both high from a really great performance. Pulling me close to him, John leaned over and began kissing and fondling me. I knew this was the time to tell him my news.

Pushing him back, I said, "Honey, I have something I need to share with you."

I was scared of what he would do or even say, but I tried to be brave and get it out at the same time. My stomach was full of butterflies. With a quiver in my voice, I looked him straight in the eyes and said, "I haven't had a period since December, and realize I am two months pregnant." The tears that had started to well up in my eyes began to roll down my cheeks. I pushed them away with the back of my hands.

It took John a few seconds to respond.

"Are you sure?" he asked anxiously, with a contorted look on his face. He was trying to grasp the information I had just given him; he was totally stunned.

"Absolutely," I responded. "Aside from having missed two periods, my breasts are starting to swell and are quite sore. I do want you to know I am prepared to have the baby and give it up for adoption."

At first, John was silent as he gathered the information I had just given him. I could see the wheels turning as he tried to think of what to say next. He was totally flummoxed, and needed time to formulate a reply. It was only seconds, but it seemed like forever.

The last thing I wanted to do was to force John to marry me. The only other options for girls who got pregnant were to be shuffled off to a relative in another town or city where they weren't known, or sent to a home for unwed mothers. Neither of those options appealed to me. I felt I was adult enough to handle it on my own.

"Obviously you've had a lot of time to think about your situation, and I must take some responsibility, too," John replied with passion in his voice. I was so relieved at his response. "Of course I will stick by you," he added. Then, without missing a beat, he said, "Honey, I know we have agreed to wait until we are more settled before getting married, but we're crazy about each other. Let's throw caution to the wind and get married now."

I couldn't believe John had said that.

"No, you don't understand. I do not want to get married now," I said. "We're not ready to take that step. It would be nice, though, if you would stand by me as I go through my pregnancy, as you said."

"Of course I will!" he replied without hesitation, spoken like the true gentleman he was.

I burst into tears as John pulled me close to him and started massaging my back. He planted kisses on my forehead, my cheeks, and finally fully on my lips. It was a relief to have finally shared my secret with him.

"If we are still as crazy about each other after the baby is born as we are now, we can get married next year," I said sincerely. "This is our secret, and I don't want to tell anyone, even our parents."

Still, I shuddered to think of the coming months.

FINDING A DOCTOR

"Dr. Papsin, I need some advice about finding a doctor. Do you have time to meet me for a coffee?"

"Sure. Let's meet in the cafeteria at 9 o'clock," he said.

John and I had chosen to live in Hamilton, knowing he could find work and live with his parents. My dad's youngest brother Dave and his wife Fran lived there, but we weren't that close. Paramount for me was to find a doctor, as I was already into my third month.

On my way into the cafeteria, I grabbed a discarded Toronto Telegram newspaper to read while waiting for Dr. Papsin, choosing a table for two at the back of the room. I was so engrossed in the paper that I didn't realize Dr. Papsin was sitting across the table from me until I heard him say, "How did John take your news?"

"Not only did he it take it like a man—he says he will be there for me throughout my entire pregnancy."

"So now you need to see a doctor," he said. "Have you thought about where you will have your baby?"

"Yes. Hamilton—it's John's hometown, and nobody knows me there."

"I'll arrange for you to see Dr. Maloney, then," he said.

Dr. Maloney was chief of Obstetrics and Gynaecology at Women's College Hospital; I didn't think in a million years she would have time to see a single nurse who had managed to get herself pregnant.

"I know she will be able to help you," he added.

"Really?" I said in astonishment.

"Yes, trust me," he assured as he patted the back of my hand. "She's a really great person. When you meet with her alone, you'll see what I mean."

With knocking knees, I entered Dr. Maloney's office in the Medical Arts building; it was the third Friday in March, 1962. The waiting room was empty.

Did I have the right day? I thought. *Was this the time Dr. Papsin told me to be here?*

I sat down and picked up *Look* magazine, glancing at all the certificates on the soft blue walls. I had an achy feeling and a churning stomach; I felt like I wanted to throw up. Without even glancing through it, I put the magazine back on the table, deciding to just sit there and wait.

Hearing a door open, I looked up to see Dr. Maloney in a white lab coat over her pale grey jersey dress. In her gravely voice and with a big warm smile she said, "Hello. You must be Jill."

"Yes," I replied, "I am. Thank you so much for seeing me."

"Come on in," she said in a friendly but gruff manner. She took a seat behind a very large mahogany desk. More certificates lined her office walls.

Dr. Maloney was a middle-aged, grey-haired, rather large woman; she had beautiful pale blue eyes and a warm and caring smile. "Do sit down," she said, pointing to the chair opposite her desk.

I sat down holding my purse tightly with both hands.

"Dr. Papsin tells me you want to move to Hamilton to have your baby. Have you any idea how far along you are? I understand you still have a couple of months left to finish your courses at university."

"Yes," I replied, "I'm at least three months pregnant. It's my intention to move to Hamilton the last week of May."

Dr. Maloney took time to ask about my studies and interests in an attempt to make me feel comfortable. She made me feel like I was not a bother and that she truly wanted to help me. Reaching for the telephone on her desk, she fingered through her Rolodex, searching for a number before she began dialling.

"Gerard," she said, running her fingers through her short, curly grey hair, "This is Gerry. I have a very nice young nurse in my office. She is single and pregnant and says she wants to have her baby in Hamilton. Can you see her within the next week or so?" They bantered back and forth like two old chums. I was relieved at the way Dr. Maloney presented my case without judgement. Before hanging up, she asked, "Would you be able to see Dr. Quigley next Saturday?"

Smiling and nodding, I said, "Yes, I can!"

Relief washed over me as I left her office clutching the information about seeing Dr. Quigley. I was beginning to feel that everything would be okay.

Exiting the elevator in the lobby, I headed for the bank of payphones and searched my wallet for a dime. Reaching John's office, I had to wait to be connected by the receptionist.

"John here," he answered. "Who is this?"

"Hi John, it's me," I said. "I've just left Dr. Maloney's office and she has arranged for me to see Dr. Quigley in Hamilton next Saturday. Will you go with me?"

"Of course—you know I will," he answered. "We can have dinner with my parents before coming back."

It was hard to concentrate on my studies while waiting for those days to pass until we left for Hamilton. At work the following Tuesday, I paged Dr. Papsin to thank him.

"See, I told you Dr. Maloney was a really great lady!" he said. "Let me know how it goes with Dr. Quigley."

Entering Dr. Quigley's office in the Hamilton Medical Arts building, we immediately sat down on one of the several chairs lining the pale green walls. A tall, handsome, fatherly man in horned-rimmed glasses walked through another door with a broad smile on his face.

"Hello, I'm Dr. Quigley," he said. "You must be Jill."

He had curly brown hair and was wearing a white lab coat over his charcoal suit.

"I am. And this is my fiancé, John."

Glancing and nodding at John, he said, "Jill, I think it would be best for you come into my office alone."

Without saying a word, John leaned over and kissed me on the cheek, turning to sit in one of the chairs lining the walls. Over his desk were at least as many certificates as Dr. Maloney, maybe a few more.

"Please make yourself comfortable," he said, pointing to the chair across from his desk. Like Dr. Maloney, he was kind and considerate. "Do you have a job to come to in Hamilton?"

A job. I hadn't even thought about a job. I just wanted to get this part over with first.

"No, getting here was my first priority," I replied anxiously.

"How would you like to work at St. Joseph's Hospital where I will be delivering you?"

Wow! First I was directed to a kind and caring doctor, and now he was offering me work!

"That would be great," I replied warmly.

He picked up the phone on his desk and, after having a brief conversation, hung up the phone. "Sister Ursula, who is head of Maternity at St. Joseph's Hospital, will see you after you leave here," he said.

I had my first pre-natal examination with Dr. Quigley that day.

"You're a healthy young woman," he said, "and from my calculations, you will deliver towards the end of September." He had put me totally at ease during the examination. Out in the waiting room, Dr. Quigley spoke briefly to John while I got dressed. Once dressed, I said to John, "Dr. Quigley has arranged for me to meet Sister Ursula today at St. Joseph's Hospital to discuss working there!" We left Dr. Quigley's office, and walked around the corner to the hospital.

"Would you please contact Sister Ursula for me?" I asked the receptionist in the Maternity wing. Only a few minutes passed before we saw a kindly-looking nun appear. She wore a habit and full-length nursing whites with shiny white nursing shoes peeking out from the bottom of her robes. Sister Ursula's angelic face put me right at ease as she extended her hand to greet me.

"You must be Jill. Dr. Quigley tells me you would like to work here until your baby is born. Is that correct?"

"Yes, that is correct. However, I cannot start until the end of May as I am still completing my public health course at the University of Toronto."

"Would you be available to start Monday May 28th?"

"Yes" I replied, "that would work out perfectly."

"Please find time to come and see me during that afternoon, and I will set up your working documents," she said. "I think it best if you work permanent nights, away from the prying eyes of the daytime staff."

"Thank you, Sister," I answered gratefully as I took my leave. Happy to know I would have work, John and I purchased a newspaper and sat on a nearby bench in the hospital lobby, searching for a place for me to live.

"This is perfect," I said as the landlord showed me around a studio apartment in an old house just a few blocks from the hospital. There was nothing fancy about it. Then again, who could afford fancy? The basics were all there. The dirty beige walls looked like they could stand a coat of paint, but I knew the place would suffice for the time I would be in Hamilton. "Does it come with any parking?" I asked.

"Yes, it's just outside the side door and is included in the rent."

Wow, parking right out in front for my 1956 turquoise and cream Plymouth Valiant with the push-button gearshift. I loved that big, beautiful car with the flowing fins at the back. Free parking—that clinched the deal.

"I'll take it," I said, shaking the landlord's hand.

As planned, we drove to John's parents that afternoon. John's father, also named John, was a chemical engineer in the nuclear reactor at McMaster University.

He greeted us from the front porch. "It's nice to see you again," he said, shaking my hand. "How is your course going?"

He was a quiet yet likeable man, and rather small—short, like John, but thinner. His brown hair with moustache and beard was slightly peppered with grey. His wire-rimmed glasses made him appear very academic.

"It's going very well," I replied. "Only two more months until it's over."

In contrast to John's father, John's mother, Henny, was a much bigger person. She had medium-length, permed, chestnut-brown hair, and beady, greenish-brown eyes. In her presence, the room often took on a distinct chill. There was nothing inviting about her. I could just feel it in my bones that she resented my relationship with her son. She was always trying to put a dent in my confidence or self-esteem. I could see clearly that the entire family cow-towed to her.

My move to Hamilton took place the last Saturday in May, 1962. My meeting Monday afternoon with Sister Ursula went well.

"Jill, I have put you on permanent nights in charge of the nursery," she said. "That way, you will have fewer people to encounter during your time with us." I released a slow breath of relief; everything was falling into place.

"Now, get yourself down to Woolworth's to purchase a cheap wedding band to go with that engagement ring," she added. "Nobody needs to know you aren't married."

"This fellow is booked for a circumcision on Thursday at eight o'clock," Kay informed me as she tucked him back into his crib. "Did Sister tell you the procedure?" In charge of the nursery on nights, Kay was my permanent health care aide.

"No," I replied, scrunching up a diaper and tossing it into the laundry bin. "You'll have to show me."

Kay was always quick to offer advice about policies and procedures in the nursery, and I appreciated her help.

"What are you knitting?" I enquired one night. We were sitting quietly doing charting in the nurses station after bottle-feeding some of the babies.

"Oh, a friend of mine has two small children, and I am knitting them mitts for Christmas." Then, with a real twinkle in her eye, she said, "Why don't I teach you how to knit? You could knit your own baby clothes!"

Kay was such a caring individual on so many different levels. Over time, I learned she had moved here from Saskatchewan with only a handful of friends in Hamilton.

"No, Kay," I responded, throwing my head back and smiling with raised eyebrows. "Knitting does not interest me in any way, but thanks for the offer."

Keeping my weight down was a number-one priority. Disguising my somewhat expanding waistline was more of a challenge. Fortunately, I had taken my trusty White sewing machine to create an entire wardrobe that did wonders for camouflaging my changing body.

Visits with Dr. Quigley became more frequent as I approached my delivery date. During one of those visits he asked, "Have you made any plans about adopting your baby?"

Of course I hadn't made any plans. What was I thinking? All I wanted to do was to have my baby and get it over with. Yes, I knew at some point I would need to contact the Children's Aid Society, but I had put it on the back burner. Rather naively, I replied, "No, I haven't."

With a twinkle in his eyes and a big smile, he said, "That's good, Jill, because I know a couple interested in adopting your baby. They've already adopted a daughter in February, but have expressed a desire to adopt another child. Would you be willing to do that?"

A private adoption! That was something that had not even entered my mind. It would be perfect. Giving up my baby to a couple who had one adopted child and were eager to adopt another was wonderful news.

Grinning from ear to ear, I replied, "I sure would!"

"Then let me speak to the couple and get the process started," he said.

"A huge load has been taken off my shoulders," I said, breathing a sigh of relief. "Now I know my baby will be in good hands. I am blessed you are taking such good care of me in so many ways."

It was not uncommon for Sister Ursula to drop by the nursery before I went off duty. "You really are looking good. You must be eating and drinking all the right things," she would tease. Then, without judgement, she'd ask, "How are you feeling?"

Sister Ursula was in her mid-fifties. She always had a smile on her face and was hardly ever was in a bad mood. No wonder she was so well-liked throughout the hospital. To me, she really was a very special person. She was always there for me, and made me feel we had a unique bond. She gave me every reason to trust her, and I did. She never blew my cover; it was assumed that John and I were married, and I would quit work when the baby was born. As far as I was aware, nobody knew any different.

The summer went by very quickly. John didn't have any trouble finding work in Hamilton, and as I suspected, he boarded at home with his parents. One Saturday in July, on my way to the farmers' market, I had called ahead to pick John up, and was surprised to see Marsha, his cute, blonde curly-haired baby sister sitting on the porch when I pulled into the driveway. As John came out of the house, Marsha looked at me with an impish smile on her face.

"Can I come with you to the market?" she asked.

Shrugging his shoulders, John replied, "It's okay with me. Get in the car and I will tell Mama you are coming along."

Marsha happily jumped into the back seat while John went back in the house to inform his mother.

At the market, we tasted food offered us by the various vendors as we selected the fruit and vegetables to purchase. On the way out, we had to pass an ice cream stand. Snuggling up to me, Marsha squeezed my hand, "Jill, can I have an ice cream cone, please?"

"Why not?" I responded. "Let's all have one."

Arriving back at John's parents for lunch, his mother was busy setting the table.

"Mama, John and Jill bought me an ice cream cone. We all had one," Marsha gushed.

John's mother's eyes bulged, and her face reddened, making her look like she was going to explode. She stared at John and launched into speaking Dutch.

From the tone of her voice, I knew she was telling him off for indulging Marsha with an ice cream so close to lunch.

"If you aren't happy we bought Marsha an ice cream cone, you can speak in English," I blurted out. "I am as much to blame as John."

Her body stiffened, and her cheeks turned pink as she turned away, wiping her hands on her apron. With venom in her voice, she said, "I didn't know you spoke Dutch."

"I don't, but it wasn't hard to figure out what you were so angry about."

Needless to say, there was none of the usual mugging by Marsha or any joking around at that lunch by anyone. I couldn't wait to leave. I was beginning to see that she was the real boss in the family.

On August 5, 1962, Marilyn Monroe died. The same weekend, Superior Propane blew up, causing a massive fire in my hometown of Maple. The following weekend, we joined my parents at Uncle Dave and Aunt Fran's BBQ. Keeping my parents at bay was really difficult as we always shared hugs and kisses when we got together. Not so this time. Instead, I clung to John. The last thing I wanted them to feel was the baby kicking if we got too close together.

"It's hard to believe that Marilyn Monroe is gone," my mother said. She continued. "Did you know that Superior Propane had an explosion the same night?" Without waiting for a reply, she added, "Herbie Joslin was the only one killed." He was the father of my elementary school chums, twins David and Peggy.

These two events stand out in my mind because it is the last time I saw my parents before I had my baby. *Do they suspect? I wondered. What are they talking about to each other?*

I saw Dr. Quigley for a regular check-up the next day, Monday, August 12th. Stepping on the scales in his office, I was up just twelve pounds. "Well, you sure are keeping your weight under control," he said. "How are you feeling?"

"I will be very happy when this is all over," I said.

As I sat up on the side of the examining table, Dr. Quigley said, "From my calculations, you will be right on time." On time meant September 27th. That was six weeks away. I was definitely getting antsy.

"I sure would like to have it over before then," I groaned, getting off the examination table.

"You'll just have to let nature take its course," he replied, patting me lightly on the back. "By the way, in order to start the adoption process, you will need to meet with Mr. White, the lawyer for the couple adopting your baby." He handed me a piece of paper. "Here is his office address and telephone number. I suggest you call him right away. All the legal bills will be covered by the adopting family." That was a real relief for me.

John arrived, as planned, for a drive to Webster's Falls before having dinner at his parents' place. It was Sunday, September 16th. It was a bright, warm sunny day with a pale blue sky and a light breeze. The leaves were just beginning to show some hints of yellow and orange. Before we ventured very far from my apartment, I started to have the most unusual back discomfort.

"John, I am not feeling great right now. My back aches and I feel slightly nauseated."

"Then I think I should take you back home," John said with concern in his voice.

"Yes please, let's go back."

I was silent all the way home.

With a worried look on his face, John asked, "Are you okay?" as he drove back to my apartment.

"I will be fine once I lie down," I said.

As soon as I opened the door to the apartment, I headed for the sofa and sat down, desperately wanting to just lie down. There was no way on earth I could make it to dinner at John's parents.

"Go ahead and take my car to your parents' place for dinner. Tell them I am not feeling well, and apologize for me. You can come back later."

I watched as John pulled out of the driveway. Suddenly, I heard a small "pop," and then there was a sensation of warm water running down my legs.

Oh my God. My water has just broken. I realized. *Now what? I can't be in labour yet.*

Dr. Quigley told me on Friday that I wouldn't deliver until the end of the month. Hurrying into the bathroom, I grabbed a towel as I attempted to wipe myself off and then mop up the mess. The pain in my back was getting worse.

Picking up the phone, I called Dr. Quigley's answering service. After explaining my situation, I asked to have Dr. Quigley call me back. Pacing the floor, I was optimistic when the phone rang that it would be him. What a relief to hear, "Hello Jill, I understand your water has broken."

"Yes, and I have excruciating back pain," I said anxiously. "I feel nauseated, but strangely, I have no contractions."

Without hesitation, he said, "Get yourself to the hospital, and I will meet you there."

Once I changed my clothes, I called John, who had just arrived at his parent's place.

"John, my water broke. I need to get to the hospital where Dr. Quigley is waiting for me. Can you make some excuse and come back to drive me there please?"

As soon as I saw the car pull into the driveway, I locked my door and got into the passenger side. At the hospital, John got out of the car and hurried to get a wheelchair for me. He came back with a nurse pushing a wheelchair. The back pain was intensifying to almost unbearable limits. I tried to hold back the tears as the nurse assisted me into the chair.

"You look very uncomfortable," she said with empathy in her voice. "You must be in a lot of distress." She turned to John. "Go and park the car," she said, "then go to Admitting."

She wheeled me directly to the delivery room.

"Where is Dr. Quigley?" I asked anxiously as I was transferred onto the delivery table. I didn't want another doctor to deliver me.

"He's scrubbing up," the nurse replied. Then I saw the door to the scrub room open as Dr. Quigley emerged.

As the nurse helped him into his sterile gown, he winked at me, saying, "Jill, I think it would be wise for you to have a general anaesthetic."

I nodded in agreement. Before I went under, I noticed the delivery room clock: it was just 7:05 in the evening.

"You have a lovely healthy baby boy," Dr. Quigley said as I awoke from the general anaesthetic.

Looking up at the delivery room clock, it was just 7:25 p.m. I didn't know whether to laugh or cry. I felt my soft tummy. It felt good. The hard bump was gone. Then, recalling the past few months of my life, I was suddenly cognizant that part of my life was behind me.

Still a bit groggy, I said, "I have a baby boy. I hope he's okay. How much does he weigh? Does he have ten fingers and toes?"

The nurse came over and stood looking down at me on the delivery table. "He weighed in at six pounds eight ounces and has ten fingers and toes. He really is cute."

It was Sunday, September 16, 1962.

AND ONE MORE THING

Sitting in the grey club chair in my green hospital room, I pushed away the over-bed table with the empty lunch dishes on it. Wearing the pale blue dress and navy cardigan John brought me to go home in, I was beginning to feel like a normal person.

"Hi, Jill," came the perky voice of Kay, who worked with me in the nursery during my pregnancy. She was a tall, dark-haired, rather buxom woman wearing tortoiseshell-rimmed bi-focal glasses. At the time, she would have been called a spinster, being in her late forties and unmarried. What was special about Kay was her warmth and kindness that shone through; when she smiled, she showed a slight overbite.

She had a large rectangular box in her hand; the box was covered in pretty baby-print paper with a big yellow bow.

What on earth is this? I thought.

Before pulling up the straight-backed chair to sit opposite me, Kay handed me the box.

"Open it! It's for you. I hope you like it."

Slowly I untied the pretty yellow bow and began removing the scotch tape at the ends of the box.

"Just rip it off," Kay exclaimed in a rather impatient voice.

Taking her advice, I ripped off all the paper and lifted the lid. Inside were a most beautiful hand-knitted baby set, a sweater, bonnet, and booties in pale green. Underneath the baby set was a baby blanket made in pale pastel squares. "I chose those colours because I knew it would work for either a boy or a girl," Kay said as I carefully lifted each item to view.

I knew she had made them, because I watched her knitting whenever she took a break while we were working. I burst into tears. What a kind gesture! I truly hoped she could not understand why I was crying. *She wouldn't know that I wasn't keeping my son,* I thought.

"I am just so overwhelmed at your generosity," I said, trying to bring on a smile. "Thank you so very much."

"Well, I'm sure he is going to have plenty of occasions to wear it," Kay commented.

"Of course he will," I replied.

"Nora has been working nights since you left on Sunday. She isn't as much fun to work with you as you were. I am really going to miss you."

We exchanged a few other words, and then Kay said she had to go catch some sleep before going on duty that night.

Do I really want to go through with giving my son up? Am I doing the right thing? These thoughts began to plague me.

I sat quietly in that chair after Kay left, contemplating those thoughts, allowing the tears to flow. In my heart, I knew the answer to both concerns was a definite *yes*.

"Good afternoon, Jill." It was the angelic Sister Ursula in her habit and long nursing whites. "Dr. Quigley tells me you are being discharged today."

"Hello, Sister" I greeted her. "It's so nice to see you."

In her calm, gentle voice, she said, "You look like you've been crying. Do you want to talk about it?"

Again, tears filled my eyes. "Sister, I am so overwhelmed at the generosity of Kay, my colleague over the past few months." Holding out the boxed baby set for Sister Ursula to see, I said, "Look what Kay has just given me. She has been knitting it since I started working with her, and I don't know what I am going to do with it. In the few short months since meeting Sister in March, I had become quite fond of her."

"I am certain there is some tiny baby who would be very happy to wear this outfit. Would you trust me to give it to that baby?"

"Of course I would. Thank you so much for being so understanding. I knew you would have an answer," I said as I put the top back on the box and handed it over to Sister Ursula. My baby was going to a couple that truly wanted him, and I knew he would have plenty of lovely clothes to wear.

"Jill, since this is your last day in hospital, would you like to see your baby?" Sister Ursula asked. *Hmmm. Do I want to see my baby?*

"Sister," I said with hesitation in my voice, "I am not so sure I should. Then again, since you have asked, perhaps I would like to see him at least this one time."

"Let me get him from the nursery," said Sister Ursula as she left my room.

When Sister returned with my son, he was in an incubator, lying on his right side, wearing only a diaper and sucking his thumb. He looked like a very healthy, happy baby with lovely pink skin and fair hair covering his perfect little head.

"Would you like to hold him?" I heard Sister ask me.

Do I want to hold him? I knew this was my only chance. Fortunately, my practical mind took over.

With all the determination I could muster, I replied, "No, Sister, I don't."

As much as I would have liked to, I knew in my heart that if I did, I would never let him go. Most of all, I didn't want to disappoint the couple who had agreed to adopt him and give him a good start in life. It was a tough decision, but I knew I had made the right one. It was time to shut that door and get on with my life.

Coming back to my room after taking my baby boy back to the nursery, Sister said, "You have one more task to complete before you leave." In her hands she waved a legal-sized piece of white paper indicating that I needed to sign. I couldn't imagine what papers I had to fill out now, because I had already signed the discharge papers. I was just waiting for John to pick me up.

"This is the official registration of your son's birth," she said.

Never in a million years did I think this task would fall to me. I thought it would be up to the couple that were adopting him to give him a name.

Have I made the best decision? Am I doing the right thing? These thoughts went through my mind yet again. Taking the form, I slowly glanced over it. At the bottom of the page was an empty space where I was to write his given name.

Through the fog of my thoughts, I heard, "Have you thought about a name for your son?"

"No, I haven't."

It never occurred to me I would have to name him However, once Sister Ursula made it clear to me that it was my responsibility, I knew exactly what it would be. Taking the black fountain pen from her extended hand, I wrote down *Robert*.

GROWING UP IN MAPLE

I grew up in Maple, Ontario. With a population of only 300, everybody knew my name. Keele Street, the main thoroughfare, was lined with big old maple trees that hung over each side of the road like a canopy. We had the standard post office, bank, hardware store, grocery and general stores, barber shop, drug store, butcher shop, one restaurant, and Texaco and BP gas stations. The protestant religion was well served with Anglican, Presbyterian, and United Churches.

Like most families in Maple, we were neither rich nor poor. We always had food on the table and clothes on our backs. Our used upright Heintzman piano arrived when I was five. As soon as I started tinkling the ivories, mother promptly enrolled me in piano lessons. A nearby outdoor skating rink was a perfect place for me to practise on my brand-new used skates obtained the year I started school. Skating lessons followed, but clearly revealed I was no Barbara Scott. We enjoyed movies in Richmond Hill, occasionally attended live theatre, and sometimes mother and I would take the bus to Toronto to hear the symphony at Massey Hall.

During the war, my father worked at De Haviland Aircraft Company assembling airplanes. He was too young to go to war in 1919 and too old in 1939. "Doris," my dad said one day after the war ended, "I want to open a restaurant." Before she could respond, he continued: "I will certainly need your blessing and help to do it."

With financial backing from my maternal grandfather, plus a local elderly man, my father began building both a house and a restaurant in 1946. To make ends meet, my mother took in boarders. We moved into our brand-new house in April 1947, and John's Coffee Shop opened in May. My parents were a team; mother was in charge of baking and soup-making, and dad was the head chef managing day-to-day operations. Together they were behind the counter, and acted as pseudo-psychiatrists, similar to bartenders of the era.

Father was a Village Trustee and an Elder at Maple United Church. Mother was a member of the Women's Institute and sang in the church choir.

"Put it on my tab" was heard regularly in the coffee shop. Never in the twenty-one years my dad operated the coffee shop did he get "stiffed" by any customers. He treated his customers with respect, and in turn, they were loyal and honourable to him.

In the beginning, the coffee shop was open from 7:30 in the morning until midnight, seven days a week. I never heard either parent complain about such a gruelling pace, because that's the way businesses operated in those days. After supper, mother would lay flat cardboard on top of a pile of pop cases with a blanket on top as a place for me to sleep, covered by another blanket, until it was time to go home to bed. Around ten o'clock, mother would wake me up, and together we would walk the few short blocks home where I would get into my pyjamas before climbing into my own bed for the rest of the night.

"Dorothy is coming to baby-sit tomorrow. I'm playing Euchre at the Community Hall," Mother informed me.

"Why do you always have to play cards every Tuesday?" I whined. To this day, I have never learned to play Bridge or Euchre. Little did I understand the importance of quality time away from work and other responsibilities.

"I'll get it," a customer said as he jumped off the stool to answer the telephone in the wooden booth. "John, it's for you," he said holding, the cylinder earpiece towards my dad who was serving another customer. Until 1952, that black Bakelite pay-telephone served us very well. It was our only telephone. To make a call, you inserted a nickel and turned the crank on the side to reach the operator so she could connect you to your call. One never knew if the operator listened into your calls, as she certainly had that advantage.

My best friend, Heather—a cute, slim, trim gal with short dark hair—lived nearby. Being on the heavier side, I always envied Heather's smallness. Her mother, Jean, a switchboard operator for Woodbridge and Vaughan Telephone Company, connected subscribers on the old pull and plug board. Visiting Jean at work, we'd hear, "Number please?" Sometimes Jean would have a conversation with the person before we'd hear, "I'll connect you now."

Party lines, although less expensive, meant waiting for a free line before making your call. Others could always "listen in" if they were careful. But if they heard, "Please get off the line," there would be a click as they hung up the phone. Thankfully, my family had a private line. Maple got rotary dial phones in 1959.

"Students, we are going to visit the Royal Ontario Museum next Friday," Miss Beatty announced to us. "Remember to tell your parents, because you may be late getting home."

I just loved Miss Beatty, my primary teacher at the Maple Public two-roomed school. She was pretty with dark shoulder-length hair, green eyes, and a beautiful smile on her brightly-painted pink lips.

"When we get there, I want you all to file out of the bus and line up inside the door," she cautioned on the day of our field trip. We gawked in awe as we chatted to each other about the huge dinosaur skeletons and other exhibits we viewed. What a thrilling trip that was!

I was first to sign up when I learned about the local Lion's Club's public speaking contest a few weeks after that visit to the museum.

"What are you going to talk about?" my father asked when I told him my plans.

"My trip to the museum," I said, waving the paper in my hand to show him I had already begun to write it.

Teachers, classmates, friends, and parents filled the community hall. I was at my best when I had an audience. Public speaking was natural for me. When it was my turn, I jumped up from my chair, anxious to find my place on the stage.

"Thank you, contestants," Mr. Kinney, our Sunday school superintendent said after all six of us had spoken. "We will now have a short break for the judges to make their decision

"Ladies and gentlemen," Mr. Kinney said, clapping his hands, "The judges have made their decision. Would Jill Neufeld please come up to the front?" Dressed in my navy tunic and white blouse, I quickly slid off my chair and headed to the front of the room. I already knew how much they liked it from the applause I received when I gave my speech.

"Thank you very much," I replied confidently as Mr. Kinney handed me a small parcel. I hurried back to my seat, anxious to open my gift, which turned out to be a collection of short stories.

"Well done, young lady," my father said, patting me warmly on the back. "We're both really proud of you."

"Mom, Dad," I said, running to the front door, "Uncle Pete and Aunt Olive are here." When I was eight years old, they were my favourite aunt and uncle, and made frequent visits to our house.

"How are you, young lady?" Uncle Pete asked, pulling gently on my braids. As soon as they came in the front door of the coffee shop, he would head over to the jukebox, dropping a coin into the slot before making his selection. The records moved around until the chosen one was placed on the turn-table. Slowly, the arm mechanism would move to the edge of the record on the turntable for the music to begin. Hearing "Third Man Theme", I would hoist myself up on one of the red leather-like stools to watch Uncle Pete reach out his hand to Aunt Olive with a warm and engaging smile. "Come on, honey" he would say as she slid off the stool into his waiting arms. With eyes closed, they would dance around the room until the record was over.

At the age of nine, I was delighted to have a bicycle of my own. Dad won it through the Lion's Club for me. It was a bright red Raleigh with shiny silver chrome fenders. It went forwards and stopped when the pedals were pushed backwards—no fancy gears. However, until I could learn how to ride it, my father rode it to the coffee shop every day.

"When can I have my own bike?" I asked my father.

"As soon as you learn how to ride it," he replied.

My favourite cousin Helen worked at the coffee shop during her summer holidays. Her parents were my mother's only brother and my dad's only sister, giving us exactly the same bloodline. Helen was a pretty nineteen-year-old with a great zest for life. Engaged to Frank, Helen was looking forward to their marriage in September. Frank, a tall, thin, quiet, good-looking man from Nova Scotia, was Head Herdsman at Fraserdale Farms in Concord. They met at the coffee shop the previous summer. Helen's bubbly, outgoing nature had appealed to the more reserved Frank. "If you were cows," Frank would tease us, "you'd be blood sisters." One day, after hearing my conversation with my dad about the bike, Helen removed her apron as soon as she finished work.

"Get your bike out. Let's go for a ride!"

Off we went to retrieve the bike for my ride on Keele Street.

"Are you sure you are hanging on?" I asked, feeling Helen at my side.

"Don't worry, you're safe with me," she said.

I remember the day I mastered riding all by myself. Helen was right by my side, running along as I pumped away on the pedals. Suddenly, I was aware she wasn't there; I turned around and promptly fell off the bike.

"Get up and ride back to me," Helen yelled from down the street. I did so with delight, proud of my accomplishment.

As soon as I was able to see over the high counter, I was allowed to wait on customers.

"Apple, raisin, blueberry, cherry, boysenberry, lemon, banana cream, coconut cream, butterscotch, and chocolate," I recited. These were the delicious pies—with the best flaky pastry— that mother baked each day. Crews from Bell, Comstock, and Hydro who were working on the 400 Highway came everyday for lunch at the coffee shop. To accommodate them, Mother set up makeshift tables of wooden tresses covered by a sheet of plywood, then covered it with heavy brown paper tacked in place to act as a tablecloth. After rhyming the pies off, the crews would tease me and ask me to do it again. I did so without a flaw.

In 1951, father decided to add a second-storey apartment to the coffee shop. The restaurant was jacked up on logs and moved forward, and the basement was dug out. When completed, it was rolled back onto the foundation. My father did most of the work laying those cement blocks for the basement, and he put up the frame to finish the second storey. He did it in his spare time while my mother (and sometimes a helper) managed the coffee shop. His only help was that of a master plasterer. When it was completed in spring of 1952, we sold our house and moved into our new home above the coffee shop.

From my bedroom window, I could see the 400 highway over a mile away.

"Hurry up—everybody is here," Heather called to remind me. Her family had one of the first black and white televisions in Maple. Friends and neighbours would drop by on Sunday nights just to watch the Ed Sullivan show.

"Shhh," the adults would say, putting their index finger to their lips. "We want to see what acts he has on tonight."

It truly was everybody's favourite. *Perry Mason,* a lawyer played by Canadian actor Raymond Burr, and *I Love Lucy,* with Lucille Ball and her Cuban husband, Desi Arnaz, were also favourites. Our first black and white television would not arrive until spring of 1958, the year I went in training at Women's College Hospital, School of Nursing.

"Do you think they will still hold the dance?"

As teenagers, those Friday night dances were the highlight of our week. Heather was concerned that the incredibly heavy rain would be a reason to cancel the dance.

"Of course they will!" I replied confidently.

"Then come on down to my place while I get ready."

"Okay—I'll be right over."

Grabbing my raincoat and umbrella, I headed out the door without rubbers. That dark and stormy Friday on October 8th, 1954, the torrential rain was coming down so hard it filled the ditches on either side of the road like a river running down both sides of Keele Street.

Heather and her mother, Jean, stood at the dry edge of the sidewalk. Looking over at them from my vantage point in the middle of the road, I didn't know what to do.

"Wait there and I'll throw you some galoshes," Jean shouted. Revving up her arm, ready to throw one, she called out, "Here it comes!"

As she let it go. I stood totally helpless, watching it disappear into the raging waters. Hurricane Hazel had invaded Maple. Needless to say, the dance was cancelled.

During summers and holidays I worked at the coffee shop. With grade ten coming to an end, I was keen to try my hand at something different, but feared my parents would feel I was deserting them. Instead of being angry or annoyed with me, my dad said, "I will speak to Andy to see if there is anything you can do at the Cattle Breeders." Andy worked full-time in the office and did bookkeeping on the side for local businesses. I was so excited when, a week later, he hired both Heather and me to work in the office, stuffing envelopes and filing.

Plucking up courage after a week on the job, I said to Heather during a morning break, "Do you like it here? I'm truly bored. It's a lot more interesting working at the coffee shop." Not sure how to tell Andy, I told my dad first. Andy was not surprised at my decision. Heather stayed on and that fall went into the secretarial program at high school.

"It's good to have you back," was my father's only comment.

"Elvis Presley is coming to Maple Leaf Gardens," my friend Carol said when she telephoned one day. It was 1956, and he was taking the world by storm. "My mother won't let me go alone. Can you come with me?"

I was happy my parents let me join her on the bus with a bunch of teenagers to listen and watch his gyrations on stage.

"I am not going to yell and scream like all the others," I said before the performance began. As soon as I heard his "Don't Be Cruel", I was so hypnotized by his voice, the outlandish costumes, and the body gyrations that I could not stop myself from joining the others as they jumped around yelling and screaming while Elvis performed on stage.

At high school in Richmond Hill, I befriended another Heather who lived just around the corner from the high school. A year older than me, she was slightly taller, with blonde hair and a twinkle in her soft blue eyes. I loved her sense of humour. Her parents, like mine, were shopkeepers who lived over the store. She liked to call me Jillybean. I called her Hedy.

Being bussed to high school meant if we participated in extra curricular activities, we missed our ride home. Luckily, I was able to go home with Heather to wait for my dad to pick me up. If several of us stayed late, we would share the $1.25 cost of the four-mile taxi ride home.

"Jill, my parents have arranged for me to go to St. Clement's all-girl's school for grade thirteen," Heather informed me in May of 1957. "I'll be a day student, so we can still be friends."

This took me totally by surprise. Never had I ever heard a peep out of Heather about such a decision. Going to a private school was costly, and it was then I realized that Heather's parents were much wealthier than mine, because mine couldn't afford to send me to a private school.

"This very large embossed envelope is for you," mother said, handing it to me. "It's from Heather's parents."

"What could they be sending me?" I asked as I tore the envelope open. It was an invitation to Heather and Primrose's Debutante party. Becoming a debutante was an enormous honour; it was a place for young society women to celebrate their coming of age. Each debutante's family was expected to host a pre-ball party where they invited the other debutantes as well as their friends. Heather and Primrose's party was held at Benvenuto Place. I knew there would be many girls from very wealthy families in attendance. It was an honour to be invited to this prestigious event, and I truly enjoyed myself.

My parents worked hard running the coffee shop. They built up customer loyalty, and in return, they received respect. They taught me that, despite life's twists and turns, the best way to manage them is to be prepared and not let little things get me down.

Maple was a safe, interesting, fun, and enjoyable place to put down roots. It also prepared me for the much larger outside world that I entered at age eighteen when I left home to become a nurse.

ROBERT

The minute I saw him slip into the second pew in the balcony that warm, spring Sunday morning, my heart skipped a beat. I was fourteen, and like all teenage girls, my hormones were raging with visions of being courted by older handsome men in shining bright armour. In all our spare time, my girlfriends and I were reading magazines like *Personal Romances and True Confessions,* filled with salacious stories to indulge our vivid teenage minds; *Glamour* magazine kept us up on the current fashion, even though we certainly could not afford any of it. We longed to be older, wiser, and sexier. All the girls thought the boys in our Sunday school class were morons. They just didn't cut it. They were too immature for us. Mrs. Wiltshire's Sunday school class always met in the church balcony.

Goodness, I thought, watching this newcomer who had just arrived in our balcony class, *where did this handsome fellow come from? He should be on the cover of a romance magazine.* None of the fellows we knew were as handsome and dashing as this one. It was clear from the reaction of the others in the class that this newcomer was unknown to all of us.

He was a tall, blond Adonis, with warm, soft blue eyes and a most engaging smile. What a stunning figure he cut in his white flannels and blue plaid shirt, showing off his gorgeous bronzed skin.

"Welcome to my Sunday school class. I'm Mrs. Wiltshire. Tell us who you are and what brings you here."

"I'm Robert, and I just live over on Dufferin Street. My friend George told me about your class."

"Thank you for coming," Mrs. Wiltshire replied, noting his name on the attendance sheet.

I was a short, stocky girl with hazel eyes and ash-blond curly permed hair. *He is so handsome. I hope nobody notices I am blushing,* I thought. I cannot recall the content of that class. I was totally consumed by his presence. Despite my gregarious, outgoing, take-charge ways, I was surprised when he sought me out to chat after Sunday school

"Hi, are you a regular here?" he asked, squinting his eyes against the bright sunlight. "Do you live nearby?" We stood face to face as we continued to chat.

"I come every Sunday," I replied enthusiastically. "I live with my parents upstairs over John's Coffee Shop at the north end of Keele Street." Hoping it wasn't far away, I asked, "Where do you live?"

"I live in the white farm house on Dufferin Street, just north of Maple side road."

"So, Robert, how come we've never seen you here before?" I asked. brushing my fingers through my hair.

"I'm a Boarder at St. Andrew's College in Aurora, and only come home on weekends." That's why we never saw him at our local high school. "Please, just call me Bob," he added.

His parents must be wealthy if they can afford to send him to St. Andrew's College, I thought.

"How did you get here today?" I asked, feeling my cheeks turning pink.

"I rode my bike. It's not that far. I parked it in the rack at the back of the church. How did you get here?"

"My bike is parked back there, too."

With trembling knees, I headed towards the bike rack with Robert walking alongside. He made me feel all tingly inside.

"Would you like to come by the coffee shop for a pop?" I asked.

"Yes, I would, but I really should be heading home. If you give me your phone number, I'll call you."

That summer of 1954, Bob and I became the best of friends. His home was just a mile away from my home, within biking or walking distance. I was definitely infatuated with this absolutely handsome fellow who was a year older than me. It's hard to recall now just how it all came together, but we hit it off from the start. We became fast friends, and he was a regular visitor at the coffee shop.

"Tell me what it's like going to an all-boy's school," I said to Bob as we sipped soda pop.

"Well, it's pretty disciplined. We have Chapel every morning before classes. The teachers are really strict and expect us to get good marks."

"It doesn't sound like any fun," I added.

"Oh, it is. We have sports and other extra-curricular activities, such as band, choir, and drama classes."

I felt my cheeks turn a pinkish hue as I listened to his story. Coming from a wealthy family and attending a private school put Bob in another realm. Despite that, he never let it get in the way of us being friends.

Elvis Presley came on the music scene in the mid 1950s, taking the world by storm and becoming an international over-night sensation. His unique and diverse music challenged social and racial barriers. As true Elvis fans, Bob and I spent hours listening and dancing to his records. Don't be Cruel was our all-time favourite, and Love Me Tender, Love Me True came in second.

As I sat practising the piano, I heard the roar of a car engine turning into our driveway, stones flying in all directions. Looking out the widow, I saw Bob in a red sports car pulling up by the front door. It was a few days after Bob's sixteenth birthday in May 1955. With such a bright and sunny spring day, it was only natural to have the top down. When I reached the front door, my parents were already there. Grinning from ear to ear, Bob turned off the engine and slowly sauntered out of the car.

"So what do you think about my brand new MG?" he asked.

I stood there with my mouth open, staring at Bob and then at the car. All I could get out was, "Wow! When did you get it?"

Without saying a word, Bob walked around to the passenger side and opened the door. "Come on, get in, I'll take you for a ride."

Trying to keep my composure, I slowly walked around to the passenger side where he stood holding the door open.

"I guarantee you will love it," he said.

As I slid down onto the warm, dark brown leather seat, I planted my legs in front of me. I had on a white blouse and green felt skirt, with two crinolines that I carefully tucked into the passenger side. On my feet were white ankle socks with my brown and white saddle shoes. Bob carefully closed the door.

"Are you comfortable?" he asked.

I was in seventh heaven. "Sure am," I replied, taken in by all the gauges on the dash.

Revving the engine, Bob put the car in gear, throwing up more stones from our gravel driveway as we roared onto Keele Street. My hair was blowing all over my face, and all I could do was giggle.

Why didn't I think about putting a bandana on to keep my hair in place?

"Isn't this just the greatest?" Bob asked, still grinning.

Of that there was no doubt. I actually felt quite smug watching local heads turn as we whizzed up and down the various streets of Maple, showing off Bob's car. A sports car like that was a real novelty to the folks in Maple.

Arriving back at the coffee shop, my mother and father were standing on the porch, relieved we had returned in one piece.

"How'd you like my new car?" Bob asked, holding the door to help me out.

As I exited the car, I slowly ran my hand over the back of the leather seat. "I love it!" I said. "When did you get it?"

"It's my parents' sixteenth birthday gift to me," he said.

Now that he had a car, I knew I'd see a lot more of Bob.

To celebrate, we had a donut and pop before heading upstairs to listen to records.

"Let's play Elvis. How about 'Love Me Tender'?" Bob suggested as he eased the 78 rpm record from the sleeve. He put it on the turntable and placed the needle on the vinyl record. "Okay—time to dance" he said, standing up and pulling me off the sofa. Giggling, we pushed the coffee table aside and tucked the piano bench in so we could dance in our rather small living room.

Holding me close while dancing sent shivers up and down my spine. Pressed into his body, I would get a warm glow all over, savouring the scent of his after-shave lotion. I just loved being with him.

As an only child, my parents encouraged me to bring my friends home. Parties were a common occurrence. Some of my friends were dating, but many were not. Word got around at how much fun my parties were, so in time, even others I did not know that well wanted to be invited.

"Do you want a hamburger or a hot dog?" my mother would enquire of my friends who stood expectantly around the brick BBQ in the back yard. "The mustard and ketchup are on the table over there," she'd add, pointing at the makeshift table near the patio as she provided the hungry crowd with sustenance. My dad did the barbequing. A galvanized tub of ice held bottles of pop.

I always suspected that my best friend Heather also had a crush on Bob. Whenever Bob's car was heard in our driveway, Heather would come over to visit. I couldn't help feeling a bit jealous, although Bob never gave me reason to believe he was interested in her.

"I have a new record for you to hear," Bob announced, running up the stairs to our apartment. Walking over to our gramophone, he turned it on and placed the record on the turntable. Next, I heard the uplifting, sunny and light sounds of Charles Trenet singing a ballad-like song in French. "It's called 'La Mer'; he wrote it. I'd hoped you would like it as much as I do."

Bob stood grinning widely, sucking in his breath through his teeth before breathing out through his nose. It made me feel warm all over, yet brought a lump to my throat. Even though I couldn't fully understand the words, I was fascinated by what I was hearing.

"I like his easy style and the lyrical flow of the music," I replied. Tucking in the piano bench and moving the coffee table to the hall, Bob gently pulled me to him as we danced around the room. His very presence kindled a slow burning flame through my entire body. I was on cloud nine. Dancing was a way to be close to Bob. Of course, when the record ended, we fell onto the sofa. Pulling me into him and kissing me full on the lips gave me goosebumps all over. Most of all, I liked that his after-shave lingered on my clothes long after he had gone.

If Bob stayed too late, his mother would call, saying, "Tell Robert it's time to come home for dinner." Laughing, he would hop into his car and drive away.

I remember the first time I met George Henderson: his family had a country farm across the concession road from Bob's place. Heather and I had biked over to Bob's. The Henderson's country home was the place to go to escape the hustle bustle of the city. George attended Upper Canada College, an all-boys private school in the city. I was quite impressed by the tennis courts at the back of the house. The only other ones I'd ever seen were at the park behind the coffee shop.

Bob frequently brought George to the coffee shop for a drink and a chat. He also brought his St. Andrew's buddies, John and Pete. Sometimes Bob would bring them to a party.

One time, Bob and George arrived when my mother was helping my father lay a sidewalk along the side of the coffee shop.

"Is your mother really helping your dad pour cement?" George asked with a quizzical look on his face. I knew if his family needed a project done, they hired someone to do it.

"Sure, my mother often helps my dad with various chores around our place," I casually replied, neither embarrassed nor apologetic.

One day, Bob, all handsome and tanned, came by in his MG with the top down. "Bob," I bragged, "I just got my 365 day licence!"

"Okay!" he said. He got out of the car and moved to open the driver's door open. "Hop in and let's see how you do."

Wow, Bob was going to let me drive his precious sports car! I knew that my first experience coordinating my hand and foot movements with a gearshift wasn't going to be easy. In fact, I was terrified I might do something wrong. Very patiently, Bob took me through all the checkpoints on the car, telling me what each gauge meant, and helped me understand the various gears. It took me a while to get the hang of the gears without grinding them, but finally I was driving south on Keele Street.

"See? You're doing just fine. It's not that hard to do, is it?" he said.

Arriving at the railway track, I put the car in neutral, got out, and went around to the passenger side where Bob was firmly planted. Looking up at me, he said, "What are you doing?"

"I don't know how to back up. If you do it for me, I'll be able to drive forward."

Tossing his head back with a big, bold laugh, Bob would hear none of it. "Get back behind the steering wheel!" he said.

With more patient instruction, I managed to reverse the car and drive back to the coffee shop with a satisfied grin on my face. I had conquered driving with a gearshift—well, maybe not conquered, but I certainly had a lot more confidence.

In June 1956, I passed my driving test on the first try. I was happy that Dad let me drive his car to Bob's place. Minnie, their live-in maid, was always hospitable to me. I remember when she overheard Bob telling me he wanted to be a lawyer. She quickly piped up, "You'll make a great lawyer, because you are such a good liar!" At the time, I wondered what she meant, but was afraid to ask Bob for fear he would be annoyed.

Taking it lightly on the chin, he quipped, "Thanks Minnie."

All the times I spent at Bob's place, I was cautious around his parents, who were kind and treated me well. However, I was always aware that they didn't think a local girl was "good enough" for their Robert.

Always a bit of a troublemaker, Bob managed to get expelled from St. Andrew's in 1956, forcing him to attend Richmond Hill high school for grade thirteen. I was in grade twelve and absolutely thrilled to have Bob at the same school.

"Bob's mother wants to speak to you," mother called up to me. It was early June, 1957. Any other time she called was to remind Bob to go home or to pick something up on his way home. This was the first time she had ever called me specifically. *I wonder why she wants to talk to me.*

"Jill," she began, "I wanted to tell you before you hear it from anyone else. Bob has gotten a girl he met a few months ago *in the family way*. You and Bob have been friends for a long time, and I wanted you to hear it from me first."

Did I hear what I thought I heard? Why isn't Bob telling me this?

"Bob will have to quit school to get married," she continued, "and will need to find a job to support his family."

Bob never told me about having an interest in anybody. I was stunned. My mind was a blur. It took me a few minutes to digest what I had just heard.

There must be a mistake, I thought.

She went on to tell me the girl had been crowned Miss Grand Bend a couple of years ago, and was older than Bob. Pete, Bob's school chum, had introduced them. (Grand Bend is a small tourist town on Lake Huron, many miles from Maple.) From the way she spoke, I could tell that Bob's mother was not pleased at this turn of events. She went on, saying, "I am sorry I didn't treat you better over the years. You are a very nice young lady, and I truly wish you the best in your future."

Bob had just turned eighteen. A quiet, family-only wedding happened a few days later. He never completed high school.

In August, Bob invited me to meet his wife. Initially, I refused. I knew it would be awkward for both of us, but he was most insistent.

"Please, Jill, you are a good friend, and I really want you to meet her."

They were living in a scantily-furnished basement apartment. His wife was an attractive young woman with blonde hair, fair skin, and blue eyes. From the bulge under her apron, she appeared to be about five months pregnant. I'm certain she felt as uncomfortable as I did. I was genuinely confused and upset at this turn of events in Bob's life. He eventually found a job working in sales and marketing in a downtown Toronto firm that made business forms.

His son, Greg, was born just before Christmas of 1957. Bob insisted I drop by to see the baby. He had dark curly hair and brown eyes—but both Bob and his wife had fair hair and blue eyes. Stunned and speechless, I couldn't get away soon enough.

Arriving at home, I immediately shared with my mother. "He looks just like Bob's friend Pete!"

"Well, Bob obviously had his finger in the pie, too," she responded, "and he got caught!"

A DIFFERENT ME

"Hi, Honey," I said to John as he came through my hospital room doorway. "Are you ready to leave?" he asked curtly. I knew it was his lunch hour.

"Yes, I'll call my nurse and ask her to take me downstairs. Where did you park?"

"I'm right out in front," he replied, looking out the window and pointing down.

Opening the door to the apartment that September 19, 1962 gave me a sense of light-headedness. I stared at the room like I didn't belong there; I felt as though doom and gloom had moved in with me. I choked back the tears, attempting to put a good face on for John. He was oblivious to my feelings. To John, everything was just fine, because as soon as I put my suitcase down and sat on the sofa, he said, "Let's go out to dinner and a movie when I get off work."

I bit my tongue, trying not to appear negative to him.

I know he is just trying to take my mind off things, I thought.

"Okay," I agreed. "That gives me time to unpack and have a nap

John leaned over and kissed me full on the lips. "See you later," he said.

I sat down on the sofa, unable to hold back any longer. My body shook as I sat there and sobbed my heart out.

What have I done? Why can't I just pull myself together?

Over dinner, John tried to keep the conversation light. I really didn't have much to say. My mind would not stop reviewing the past few months since I arrived in Hamilton.

Now it is all over and I need to get on with the rest of my life.

John picked *The L-Shaped Room* with Leslie Caron, knowing we both enjoyed foreign films—however, we were oblivious to its content. As the story unfolded, we learned it was about Jane, a young, unmarried, pregnant French woman who moved to England to live in a run-down boarding house, each resident a social outsider in his or her own way. Her room was the L-shaped room. She started a romance with Toby (Tom Bell) one of the residents, a writer. That was quickly disrupted when he found out she was pregnant by a previous suitor. When she went into labour, the other residents were there for her. Toby then visited Jane in hospital and gave her a copy of the book he'd written, titled *The L-Shaped Room*. Jane eventually traveled back to France, leaving behind the room she inhabited for seven months.

Needless to say, I bawled my eyes out all through the entire movie, but sat mesmerized by it and didn't want to leave. On top of that, my milk had started to flow, throwing my emotions into overdrive. I became acutely aware of how easy one can fall into postpartum depression. My emotions ran the gamut from the depths of despair, with uncontrollable crying jags, to fits of giddiness.

Noticing how affected I was by the movie, John said, "Do you want to leave?"

Shaking my head, I replied, "No, I want to see what happens in the end." My handkerchief was wringing wet, as was the sleeve of my navy blue cardigan.

The process of returning to my former life was not going to be as simple as I had originally imagined. Having experienced the joy and excitement of giving birth changed my thinking and put me into an entirely new realm. I had returned to my former self, but as a new model, equipped with a great deal of new attitudes and ideas. It was like taking on an alteration in my basic personality. *Who am I now?* I wondered.

TWISTS AND TURNS

My time in Hamilton was over. It was time to move back home with my parents in Maple. John remained in Hamilton until he could secure work in Toronto. Getting my life back together was not going to be easy.

There was one last trip to see Dr. Quigley for my postpartum visit in the middle of October. After my examination, I met Dr. Quigley in his office to wrap everything up. As I got up to leave, he asked, "Jill, have you found work yet back in Toronto?" "Not yet" I replied, surprised.

"My sister, Anne Marie, is head of St. Elizabeth's Visiting Nurses Association. Why don't I arrange for you to meet with her?"

First Dr. Quigley found a family to adopt my baby, and now he wanted to help me get a job.

A few days after that visit, I met with Miss Quigley.

"Gerard tells me you have completed your public health nursing and need to secure work back in the city," she said. It was more of a conversation than an interview. I tried to be positive during my time with Miss Quigley, unsure of where the conversation was going.

Then, out of the blue, she said, "Jill, I am terribly sorry, but I cannot hire you, because you are not Roman Catholic."

Why didn't Dr. Quigley tell me that before I came to meet his sister? I wondered. It had never crossed my mind that all St. Elizabeth visiting nurses had to be Roman Catholic. "However," Miss Quigley went on, "a colleague of mine is Director of Nursing at Scarborough General Hospital. I am certain she would have something for you. Can I set up a meeting with her?"

"Yes, I would be most pleased to meet with her," I responded enthusiastically. "Thank you so much!"

My interview at Scarborough General Hospital a few days later went well, and I was hired as an Assistant Head Nurse in the emergency department.

I had never discussed my pregnancy with anybody, including my mother. Arriving home that rainy November day in 1962, I hurried through the coffee shop to head upstairs to our apartment. Glancing at the notepad beside the telephone, I saw three names in my mother's handwriting—my obstetrician, my lawyer, and my anaesthetist. They jumped off the page at me. First, I just stared at the page in total shock. Then my heart sank to the bottom of my feet. I stood glued to the floor, trying to get my thoughts together.

How could this have happened? What does my mother know?

My secret was out.

Has Mother known all along? I wondered.

Tearing the top sheet off the note pad, I went into the kitchen where my mother was busy making pies. I held the note up. "Where did you get this information?"

Wiping her hands on her apron, Mother looked at me, shaking her head. "John's mother called today," she said. "She found your anaesthetic bill in John's raincoat pocket."

Why would she go through John's pockets? She too must have known all along, I thought.

Frightened and curious, I said, "What did you say to her?"

"I told her it was your baby and you could do whatever you wanted with it." Of course, my mother did not know the sex of my baby. How could she? We'd never had that conversation. She didn't lecture me or tell me my choice was right or wrong. She had, in her own inimitable way, stated her case to John's mother, and that was that. Clearly, Mother knew all along I was pregnant, but honoured my decision not to discuss it. The very fact that John's mother had the audacity to go through John's coat pockets made me realize that she had also suspected.

WEDDING PLANS

After moving back home, I was delighted to have John spend every weekend with me in Maple. Shortly after the cat was out of the bag, he had a decided spring in his step. This was evident one day as he got off the bus on a Friday in late November 1962. Coming through the front door was a broadly beaming John.

"My dear, let's set a wedding date," he said.

It came totally out of the blue, taking me completely by surprise. Despite being engaged, setting a date was a commitment we had put on the back burner.

Not sure how to respond, I asked, "What brought that on?"

"It's been on my mind a lot. It's time we made it happen." Together that evening, we decided on September 7th which was less than a year away. Excited at our decision, we told my parents.

"Well, I'm glad you're going to make an honest woman of her," my father said with great concern in his voice. Mother, ever the optimist, got up and hugged and kissed me, then did the same with John.

"That is good news. I am truly happy for you both."

Later, while watching television, I began to ruminate over our decision. Turning to John, I asked, "Are you absolutely positive about getting married?" *Hmm. . .am I having second thoughts?*

"I wouldn't have suggested it if I weren't totally positive," he said.

Over the rest of fall and winter, John continued to visit every weekend, and on Wednesday evenings, he would telephone me. Despite the fact that it was a long-distance call, we unabashedly declared our love for each other.

"My Dear, I've secured a position at a stock brokerage company in Toronto," John informed me that spring of 1963. "Now I will need to find accommodation there."

Aunt Lil, who lived in north Toronto, took in boarders. I learned she had a spare room, and I was pleased that John decided to take it.

Arriving home after work one Friday, in late March 1963, Mother handed me an envelope. "It's from the Hamilton Children's Aid Society. You might want to take it upstairs to read by yourself."

Good advice. I sat on the sofa and opened the envelope. It contained a cover letter with an attachment, and a stamped return envelope. It was the final adoption papers. I could taste the salt as the tears rolled down my cheeks, over my lips, and onto my lap. I was jolted out of my daydream when I heard John running upstairs as my mother shouted, "John's here!"

With moist eyes, I greeted John with hugs and kisses before pulling him onto the sofa with me.

"You've been crying. What's wrong?"

"Honey," I said, handing the letter to him, "Children's Aid has sent the final papers for me to sign off on the adoption."

I watched John rub his temples absentmindedly as he read the letter and enclosed document. Pulling me close to him, he begged, "Don't sign the papers. Let's get married now and get our son back."

Stunned at his response, all I could say was, "John, you don't understand. I made an agreement last summer to give up this baby to a couple who truly wanted him. I will not disappoint them by asking them to give him up now. End of conversation!" Taking the ballpoint pen off the coffee table, I carefully signed my name in the assigned place. After putting the document into the return envelope, I licked it closed, running my hand across the back to ensure it was sealed.

With an upcoming wedding, my father made plans weeks in advance to paint the outside of the coffee shop over the Victoria Day long weekend. As John and I sat chatting on the patio that Sunday afternoon, we heard the arrival of a car. Next, doors were slammed shut. We were all flabbergasted to see John's parents and his two sisters arrive without any previous warning. Annoyed, I turned to John and asked, "Why didn't you tell us your parents were coming here this weekend?"

Throwing up his hands in the air, John replied with a surprised look, "They didn't tell me a thing! Their arrival has me as perplexed as the rest of us!"

Always gracious, my mother suggested they join John and me on the patio where she would bring out some cookies and cold drinks. My father, way up the ladder, continued with his painting.

Looking up at my father, John's mother beckoned, "Aren't you going to join us?"

"This is the only time I have to get this done, and I am not stopping now" was my father's gruff reply.

"We've come all the way from Hamilton, and you are totally ignoring us!"

"Think whatever you want. You weren't invited. I have work to do."

As soon as she and the girls finished their cold drinks, John's mother stood up curtly, saying to her husband, "John, hurry up and finish your drink. We're leaving."

Undeterred by the behaviour of John's mother, my father continued painting. When he got down from the ladder and found me alone, he asked, "Are you sure you want to marry this guy?" I'd always suspected that my father was not too keen on John.

What an honour it was to be feted with a community bridal shower in mid-June with over 100 in attendance.

"Mom, I can't believe I have so many fabulous gifts," I said. "We'll hardly have to purchase anything for the kitchen or bathroom!"

"You really are a very lucky girl," Mother commented. She shook her head, looking over all the gifts.

"Wow, I sure have a lot of thank-you notes to write."

Answering the phone at the beginning of July, I was happy to hear it was my friend Heather from Richmond Hill.

"When are we having the next fitting for our bridesmaid dresses?" she asked.

"I spoke to Mrs. Ammert last week, and she wants to have them all at the same stage before we go over there. Joan will have to come up from the city, so I will see if we can do it next weekend." Our final fitting was the end of July.

"I just love my pretty mauve dress," Vickery, my flower girl, squealed with delight.

"You do look lovely in it" Mrs. Ammert noted. After all the *oohs* and *ahhs* about how we all looked together, we thanked Mrs. Ammert for her excellent skill in making these attractive dresses. I just loved how beautiful the tulip lace fitted over the champagne *peau de soie* on my dress. It was perfect.

The first week in August, John made his regular mid-week call. I had already stopped working to prepare for our wedding. With excitement, I told him about how great the dresses looked.

"I guess it's time I made arrangements about the tuxedos when I am back in Toronto," he said. The conversation went on for just a few more minutes as we were both conscious of the cost for a long distance call.

"Jill, I'm calling to tell you I won't be seeing you this weekend. I want to spend time with my parents, and hope it won't upset you so close to our wedding."

"That's okay with me. I hope you enjoy your time with your family."

"I love you very much," John declared before hanging up.

I busied myself writing thank-you notes and enjoyed quiet time with my parents. I expected John would call sometime over the weekend, but when he hadn't by Sunday evening, I became concerned. Expressing this to Mother, she replied, "Oh, he probably decided to take the bus in to work tomorrow. He'll likely call you from the office." It certainly sounded plausible.

By Monday noon, he still hadn't called. Panic set in.

"Mom, I have a strange feeling that something isn't right. I'm going to call him at work."

As I made the long distance call to John's office, I started to feel light-headed with a tightness in my chest. When I heard the receptionist answer, I asked if I could speak to John.

"I'm sorry," she answered, "John no longer works here." *Not working there?* I was dumbfounded and caught totally off-guard. My mind began going over the events of the past week. There was nothing to suggest John was unhappy at work. In desperation, I asked, "May I speak to his supervisor?"

I was put on hold, then heard, "Mr. Simmons here."

"Hello Mr. Simmons, this is Jill speaking. I'm trying to get in touch with John."

I could hardly believe my ears when I heard, "John no longer works here. He gave his notice two weeks ago."

I was totally gob-smacked. I felt cold all over. My body started to shake. I felt like I had been swallowed up into a great big hole.

Where is he? Why did he quit? Why didn't I know about this?

With a hushed "Thank you," I hung up the phone.

I just stood there. I was absolutely distraught at the realization I had been jilted. I pulled out the chair from the telephone table and sat down with my head in my hands. It was like being in a dream that would be over when I woke up. My world as I knew it had just crashed completely without warning.

Remembering my mother was in the kitchen, I opened the door and walked towards where she was working.

"John quit work on Friday and left no forwarding address."

Tears streaming down my face, Mother gently held me in her arms.

"Quit work? What do you mean?" she asked.

"He gave notice two weeks ago!"

"Jill, this is just terrible. What a coward! Perhaps Aunt Lil might be able to shed some light on the matter."

When I was certain Aunt Lil would be home from work, I made the call.

"Hi Aunt Lil. Have you seen John today?" I asked.

"No, I usually leave for work before he gets up. As a matter of fact, I haven't seen him since last Thursday night. Let me go up and check his room."

Returning to the phone, I could hear that she was slightly out of breath. "The bedroom is bare," she said in surprise. "There is not trace of John anywhere!"

"Oh my goodness!" I blurted out. "What could have happened to him?" Hanging up the phone, I turned to Mother. "He has totally disappeared!"

Hurt, heartbroken, and angry, I tried to put the pieces together. "Mom, I'm going to call Don," I said. John's best friend Don was to be our best man.

As soon as I heard his voice, I blurted out, "John quit work on Friday, has moved out of my aunt's house, and left no forwarding address. Do you have any idea where he is?"

"What do you mean quit work?" Don queried.

After explaining my findings to Don, he said, "Have you called his parents?"

"No, and I don't want to. Would you do that for me please?" I begged.

Waiting for that call seemed to take forever. When Don called back, he said, "They said they knew nothing and hung up. Jill, I am so sorry. How terrible this must be for you!"

"Thanks for making the call. I am absolutely certain his mother is to blame, but John went along with it," I said.

Crushed and angry at being jilted by John, I recalled the many times John's mother and I clashed. However, I didn't think she would stoop so low to prevent us from getting married.

PHOTO MEMORIES

Maple Public School 1948 (I am 3rd from left, second row, Miss Beatty upper left)

My Raleigh bike 1949

Heather & me on steps at coffee Shop 1952

Robert and new MG 1955

Heather, Bob and me 1955

Heather, Bob & George 1956

Heather from Richmond Hill 1956

Me 1957

John's Coffee Shop

My parents John & Doris 1961

Leo & me reconnecting 1997

Our wedding 2002

My mother's 95th 2007

First meeting, Andrew & me 2010

Robert, Sandi, Andrew, me & Victoria 2011

Kim & me, Stockholm 2011

Peggy, Margaret & me 2012, still friends after all these years

Victoria & me 2012

Mother's Day Flowers, 2014 (Robert & Andrew in back, Jill, Victoria & Sandi front)

THE HIPPIE YEARS

My Grey Cup party was in full swing that November of 1964 when a loud knock was heard at the door. Jim Fleming, one of my guests who worked at Radio Station CFRB, opened the door. He was staring at two Toronto policemen, hats in hand with sober looks on their faces. It was a wonder anyone heard the knock over the din from the revellers celebrating the Grey Cup win that day. The room was full of happy people who had come to watch the tournament on TV. The aroma of hearty chilli cooking on the stove wafted throughout the room. "We've had complaints from your neighbours, both in this building and the one next door. You'll have to tone it down," they said.

Staring at his watch, Ralph Errington exclaimed, "It can't be eleven o'clock yet!" Then, in disbelief, he looked up and said, "Oh my gawd, it's only seven o'clock!"

Clapping his hands to quiet the crowded room, Ralph had already turned the volume down. Jim invited the officers to come in and circulate amongst the revellers. We were pleased they accepted his invitation. After chatting with the guests for a few minutes, they quietly headed for the door.

We gave a low-sounding cheer as they left, saying, "Try to keep it to a dull roar."

The mid-sixties, known as the hippie years, had a tremendous influence on fashion, culture, music, arts and the embodiment of eastern philosophy. The Yorkville area became famous for its nightclubs and "the Trailer," a temporary clinic for treatment of venereal disease. St. George Street was "the place" to live. It was a time of flower children, Rochdale College, and marijuana.

The hurt and anger I initially felt at John's disappearance nearly two years before had slowly dissipated as I put my life back together. It wasn't easy. While shopping one day, I ran into Sheila, a Women's College Hospital nurse who worked at the Central Registry of Graduate Nurses.

"Hi Jill. Nice to see you! Where are you working these days?"

Withdrawing eye contact and slightly lowering my head, I said, "Actually Sheila, I am looking for work."

"Why not join the Registry?" Sheila replied cheerfully. "You get the cases from us, but you are really self-employed." Pulling out her pen and a piece of paper, Sheila asked for my telephone number.

I joined the following week. Working for the Central Registry of Graduate Nurses gave me lots of flexibility and freedom to get on with my life. By 1964, the utter humiliation of John's disappearance was behind me.

"Jill, I've met and fallen in love with George. He proposed almost immediately, and we're getting married!" my friend Phyllis announced. "However, it means I won't be going to Europe with you. I hope you won't be too upset with me." Totally undaunted, I went on my own as planned in September of 1964. After a six-week whirlwind tour of Britain and Europe, I returned home to strike out on my own.

I was delighted to find a spacious bachelor apartment on St. George Street. Most of the tenants in the building were twenty-something newly-graduated young professionals embarking on new careers. I felt I had arrived. Mr. and Mrs. Plummer, father and stepmother of Christopher Plummer, the actor, lived at the end of our floor. They were the oldest people in the building. It was a great place to live. Life was one giant party!

At last I could now put my own decorating style to work. Before going to Europe, I purchased a beige brocaded bed sofa with the realization I would have to settle for a bachelor apartment on my return. It went perfectly with the Italian Provincial coffee and end tables I purchased on sale at Eaton's College Street store. The dark walnut dining set with matching faux white leather seats fit nicely under the large expanse of northern windows. A triple dresser camouflaged as a buffet and housed my black and white TV. My brand new phonograph was being purchased "on time". Posters and inexpensive prints graced the neutral beige walls, characteristic of all apartment walls of the time. I really liked my neighbours, Bev and Trudy, who hailed from Brantford, Ontario.

It was not uncommon to be invited to an impromptu get-together put on by many of the interesting people who lived there. Dan Niosi, whose father was the famous orchestra leader known as "the King of Swing", lived a few floors down from us. "If you come by on Saturday afternoon, you can peel potatoes for my homemade vodka."

Who could refuse? It turned into a party that lasted well into the night.

Exiting the elevator that spring day in 1965, I could hear the phone ringing in my apartment at the end of the hall. Not wanting to miss the call, I ran as fast as I could, hoping the person at the other end would let it ring a few more times. Finally, I turned the key in the lock and rushed to pick up the telephone. Breathlessly I said, "Hello?"

"Hi Jill, it's John. I'm at the St. George subway and very much want to see you."

I was stopped in my tracks. I felt tightness in my chest, then everything became a blur.

John. What's he doing here?

Trying to process my thoughts, I was reminded of the rage I felt when he literally abandoned me a month before our wedding. What could he possibly want now? Then, from the depths of my mind, memories of the good times we shared jolted me into reality. How had he managed to find me? I wasn't listed in the telephone book yet. I didn't know what to say, so he just kept on talking.

Finally, after listening to him for what seemed like hours, I firmly said, "I really don't want to see you."

"Please" he begged, trying to sound sincere. "I really want to see you. It's important to me."

I struggled for a few seconds, vacillating back and forth as to why I should see him. Perhaps I might learn why he took the coward's way out when he disappeared into thin air nearly two years ago. "You can come up, but wait at least a half hour before you arrive," I said.

"Okay, I will see you in a half-hour," John said cheerfully.

Immediately, I called my neighbour Bev at work. "John, my old fiancé is at St. George subway station and is coming to my apartment," I said. "Please come home and stay with me until he leaves. I don't want to be alone with him. Get a cab and I will reimburse you for it."

Bless her soul—Bev agreed, arriving at my apartment just as the buzzer sounded, announcing John's arrival.

Opening the door to his knock, I was taken by surprise—John looked good. In the old days, my heart would skip a beat whenever we got together. Not now. The unease of seeing him gave me shivers.

Slipping out of his coat, I could see he was looking over my shoulder at Beverley, so I quickly stepped in. "John, this is my neighbour Beverley. I've asked her to stay with me while you are here. I just didn't want to be alone with you."

"Nice to meet you," he said, extending his hand. With a look of bewilderment on his face, he slumped into the single chair as Bev had already perched herself on the far end of the sofa.

"How about a coffee?" I asked, trying to sound jovial.

"A coffee would be great," John replied. Unable to think of anything to say, Bev just nodded in agreement.

What is he doing here? Why did I agree to see him?

I was pleased that John and Bev were able to manage a rather stilted conversation while I busied myself in the kitchen.

Although I was anxious to hear his story, I needed time to get myself together. "I found some cake to go with the coffee," I said, putting everything on the coffee table. I sat down beside Bev. The scene was awkward for all of us. Finally, after idle chat-chat, John put down his coffee cup. "You probably wonder why I am here," he began. "What I did was unconscionable. It has haunted me continuously since I left you. I cannot stop thinking about what we have been through together. You are such a wonderful person, and I treated you so badly. Most of all, I still love you very much." He showed remorse with the way he carefully chose the words and phrasing.

Bev just sat there staring into space, scrunching up and opening up her paper napkin. Watching her made me feel bad for putting her in this awkward situation. Had John assumed I had put my life on hold, awaiting his return?

"You still love me!" I almost spat at him. "You abandoned me without any warning!" I could hear the bitterness in my voice. "Did you get cold feet? Have you any idea how embarrassing it was for me to face all those people when I had to tell them the truth that I was jilted by you? You took a coward's way out!" As I spoke, memories of our days together came flooding back, making me a bit teary. Was it the fond memories or the anger that was making me feel this way? After all, it was true—we *did* have wonderful times together.

Sheepishly, John said, "Truly, I am so sorry, and that is why I had to see you now. I think about you all the time. I reluctantly agreed to go home to Hamilton that weekend, knowing my mother had arranged for me to go to live with friends of hers in Edmonton. She did not want me to marry you. I didn't have the guts to stand up to her."

Hearing him say that confirmed what an absolute controlling bitch his mother really was! The hostility I always felt from her was undeniable.

"How on earth did you find me?" I asked, knowing I could never trust him ever again. For me, the love we once shared was long gone. That part of my life was over. His being there was starting to get under my skin. I was anxious for him to leave, but needed to know how he managed to get my telephone number.

"A friend called your parents who gave it to him. Without you, my life is empty. I need and want you back. I have come to terms about my domineering mother. It was foolish of me to let her ruin the love we shared. Despite all that, I still love you, and am here to beg you to take me back. We could start all over again. Please rethink your response."

Throwing my hands up in the air, I jumped up. "You've got to be joking!" I exclaimed. "Did you think I was just pining away, waiting for your return?"

"I truly hoped that maybe, after hearing how much I still love you, you would reconsider," he said, sounding contrite.

"John, you had your chance and blew it," I said. I knew it wasn't the response he expected, and I could see he realized I had moved on. He had hardly touched his coffee, but we both knew it was time for him to leave.

After putting on his overcoat with careful deliberation and timing, I could see he was trying to find a way to say good-bye. Accepting rejection was not his strong suit.

Opening the door for his departure, John turned to Bev. "It was nice meeting you. I think you are a good friend to Jill, and I hope you weren't too embarrassed being here."

He then tried to muster a smile as he leaned towards me, placing a kiss on my left cheek. "I'm sorry, and I still really do love you," John whispered in my ear just before he left.

That time with John brought back memories and thoughts of Robert. Nearly two years had passed since I signed those final adoption papers. *Does he look like John or me? He must be walking and talking by now. Does he have any more siblings?* I knew he had an older sister. But it was time to move on. I had never faltered in my decision to give him up, knowing he was with a couple that really wanted him. Seeing John again merely confirmed I made the right decision. We never would have worked out. John didn't have the fortitude to be a husband and a father. It wasn't meant to be.

I shook my head at the sound of the door closing on that chapter of my life. I turned to Bev.

"Scotch on the rocks."

"You bet," she said.

THE SEVENTIES

I made a conscious decision to give up my child because I knew it would give both of us a better chance at life. That doesn't mean I forgot about him. That haunting curiosity of wanting to know that he was safe and secure never went away. The sound of a child's laughter or seeing young families together brought back speculation of what would have happened if I'd kept my son.

Working as a Rehabilitation Officer and Social Worker at Toronto East General Hospital from 1966 – 1975, I was surrounded by women with young children.

"My baby-sitter just cancelled. Now Allen and I won't be able to have our movie date," one of the physiotherapists lamented.

Hearing her angst, I volunteered. "Why don't you bring Timmy to my place on your way out and I'll look after him for you? I'd be delighted to help out."

I often baby-sat for my friends and colleagues, always hopeful that one day I would have a house full of kids—but Mr. Right always eluded me.

During Christmas 1968, I organized a basket for a less fortunate family. Patients and staff in Rehabilitation Medicine contributed both food and toys. What a pleasure it was to see the faces and hear the giggles of the four young children when we delivered to the recipients our overflowing baskets. Looking at how each child was reacting to our visit and Christmas basket made me wonder about Robert's Christmases and the joy he had opening his presents.

The orthopaedic office became a beehive of activity when, in 1969, Peggy was hired as secretary. She had medium-brown hair that framed her slightly chiselled, attractive face, and had warm brown eyes that sparkled when she spoke. Peggy had a bubbly personality, but even at twenty-one, she was rather naïve. Everyone loved her eclectic take on life.

Getting off the elevator on the Operating Room floor, I noticed Dr. Simmons had just picked up the phone in the hall. Being in OR scrubs, he held the phone away from his ear, making it easy for me to hear both sides of the conversation.

"Sir, I can't find the Thomas Rennie file," Peggy was asking on the other end of the line.

"Peggy, Thomas Rennie is a ferry," said Dr. Simmons, laughing.

"Well, sir," she said cautiously, "I don't care about his sexual orientation—I just want to know where the file is."

Laughing so loud he was almost crying, Dr. Simmons replied, "It's a boat that takes people from the mainland to the Islands. Just book it!"

By spring of 1969, Peggy began wearing a lab coat over her street clothes, trying to hide her thickening waistline. *Could she be pregnant?* I wondered. My suspicions were confirmed when she took me aside one day. "Can you keep a secret?" she asked. With trepidation in her voice, she went on: "I'm six months pregnant."

Trying to sound surprised, I said, "Really? What are you going to do? Have you made any plans yet?" Immediately, I thought about how uncomfortable I had been when I was in the same situation. "How are you feeling being single and pregnant?"

"I'm scared! I don't want to tell Ken. We broke up a couple of months ago. My Aunt Ann knows, and she has agreed to raise my baby as her own. I am too scared to tell my parents."

Now it was my turn. "Peggy, I went through the exact same thing when I was twenty-two, and gave up a son for private adoption." My mind was again filled with thoughts of Robert. Sharing that information with Peggy created a bond that brought us much closer together. I met Margaret, secretary to the Chief of Pathology, during a coffee break one day. We hit it off right away. She was a tall, blonde, flirtatious British gal who, like all of us at the time, was keen to meet her knight in shining armour. Margaret, Peggy, and I are still friends to this day.

Realizing she was in labour, Peggy tidied up the office, called her doctor, and walked up to the delivery room. Together with her Aunt Ann, they named her son Duncan.

Her spontaneity, joie de vivre, and outgoing personality were sorely missed when, instead of returning to the orthopaedic office, Peggy went to work in Dr. Simmons's private office. Life in the orthopaedic office was never the same again.

Many times, I'd heard Margaret and Peggy joke about going to Barbados. I was rather surprised one day when, while having coffee with Margaret, she announced, "I'm leaving for Barbados in the fall. Do you know anybody who wants to buy my car?"

"Are you going on your own?" I enquired.

"Well, Peggy talks about going, but I'm not sure she will follow through."

A couple of days later, Peggy joined us at lunch. Afterwards, we watched Margaret play tennis with one of the doctors. When Margaret came off the court, Peggy said to her, "I've decided to go to Barbados with you." It just came out of the blue and took me totally by surprise.

"What on earth are you going to do there?" I asked.

"Nothing," Margaret confessed, "I have enough saved for at least six months."

"Well, I might not be able to stay that long," Peggy admitted. A few weeks later, they were on their way.

Sickness brought Peggy home first. She moved home with her parents after a long hospital stay. A few months later, Margaret came back.

"Do you know any apartments for rent?" Margaret asked me shortly after her return.

She was already staying with me in my large one bedroom in St. Jamestown. "Would you like to stay here and share the rent with me?" I asked.

"That would be terrific!" Margaret responded, jumping up from the sofa and hugging me. We were officially roommates.

I met a nurse named Maggie shortly after I joined Westwood Sailing Club in summer of 1970. I was delighted to learn she worked for Dr. Papsin, who was by then Chief of Obstetrics and Gynaecology at Mt. Sinai Hospital. Once I got to know her, I told her how helpful Dr. Papsin had been to me.

"Do you think he would see me as a patient?" I asked her one day when we were waiting to take the ferry to the mainland.

"Jill, I'm sure he would."

A few weeks later I had an appointment with him.

"Jill, what a pleasant surprise to see you. Over the years I have often wondered how you are and what you are doing, then Maggie informed me she had booked you this appointment. Now tell me, how are you ?"

I took the time to tell Dr. Papsin what had transpired after I had my baby. "From the look of you I can see that you've managed to get your life nicely back in order."

Once my examination was completed, Dr. Papsin said, "See you in my office." Entering his main office, Dr. Papsin welcomed me with an outstretched hand and a big warm smile on his face. "Everything is just fine. Rose can book to come back in a year."

One Friday evening in the spring of 1971, Margaret and I were preparing for a party in our apartment when the doorbell rang.

"Who could that be?" Margaret shouted from the kitchen. "I thought you said people wouldn't arrive until after eight o'clock."

Putting on the final touches of makeup, I said, "Push the buzzer to find out."

"Is Jill there?" said a voice over the intercom. My heart skipped a beat—it was Bob. Although we casually kept in touch over the years, I was pleasantly surprised to have him show up out of the blue.

"It's Robert. Let him in," I called out to her.

"Who's Robert?" Margaret asked. I quickly explained that he was an old friend from my teenage years who was now married. "From time to time, he pops into my life. I guess we are what you might call old friends."

"Married? Well, what is he doing here now?" Margaret asked crisply.

"Just dropping by, I suspect."

Hearing his knock, I opened the door to a broadly grinning Bob. There was just something about him that commanded acknowledgement of his arrival and his presence filled the room.

"Hey, it looks like you're having a party. Got room for one more?"

How could I refuse? I was quite excited he had come to visit and wanted to hear more about him.

"Sure," I replied. He brushed by me, all eyes on Margaret. I knew he'd had affairs over the years—he'd shared that with me, though he'd never hit on me. I could see right away that Margaret appealed to him.

He handed me the keys to his car. "Since I'm staying, I'll need to park my car," he said. "Do me a favour and park it for me while I get to know Margaret better. It's in the front driveway."

When I got downstairs, I looked at Bob's ginger-coloured Lincoln Continental Luxury Mark IV parked right outside the front door. *My God, it's enormous!* I thought. With great care, I opened the driver's door and slid onto the soft, beige leather seat. I was driving a Chevy Nova. Before I put the key in the ignition, I adjusted the seat and checked all the mirrors. I was so proud I was able to park the car easily by carefully manoeu-vring it between two large round cement pillars. Returning to the apartment, I smiled broadly as I handed Bob his keys. "Nice car! Piece of cake!" I said.

"Thought you'd like it," he replied.

The guests seemed to enjoy themselves as they chatted, danced, and ate the food we put out. With a gin and tonic in hand, I sat down on the sofa. Bob approached and gestured to the vacant space beside me. "Mind if I join you?"

"Of course not," I replied enthusiastically. Bob was still very handsome and appealing, with a touch of grey on the temples of his blond hair. His provocative, musky aftershave made him smell so very masculine. It was fun just chitchatting to get caught up again. Then out of the blue, the words were out of my mouth before I realized it. "Greg is not your son, is he Bob?"

Oh my God, have I blown our friendship? I thought.

Bob leaned over and took my hand in his, making me feel tingly all over. "Jill," he said, "you are the only one of my friends who has ever had the guts to say the very thing that's been on everyone's mind. The rest think it but keep their mouths shut."

"If you're angry with me, I fully understand," I said.

"No, I'm not. I couldn't ever be angry with you. I'm relieved it's out in the open, at least with us."

It was the perfect opportunity to tell Bob about Robert, but I let the moment slip by. I didn't want to get emotional, and knew for sure I would. However, it did bring back a longing to know how my son was doing. I always had a desire to know more about him. Shortly after, Robert quietly got up, leaned over and kissed me lightly on the cheek, and softly said,

"Goodnight. It was nice seeing you again." He left without hitting on Margaret.

The two years we spent as roommates provided Margaret and me the joy of sharing many activities such as tennis, sailing, parties and day-long car trips. However, when I enrolled in a Social Service Administration course at Ryerson in 1972, I knew I needed my own space to study.

"Margaret, now that I'm back at school, I want to be on my own again. I've found a one-bedroom duplex to move into when the lease is up in two months. I hope you're you okay finding yourself a place to live."

Easing herself into a nearby chair, I could see her begin to slowly digest what I had said. "I really don't have a choice, do I? Well, I guess I can find a place to call home by the time we have to vacate this apartment."

We both moved the same day, and our friendship has never wavered.

In early spring of 1974, Margaret invited me to brunch. I should have suspected there was a reason for the invite. Sipping our coffee and relaxing at the end of the meal, Margaret put her cup down. Leaning towards me, she said, "I've decided to move back to England."

Wow, that sure took the wind out of my sails. It was totally out of the blue. I felt sad at losing my friend. I thought of all the fabulous times we shared over the years. She would be moving to another country.

"What prompted that decision? I thought you were happy in Toronto."

"I just think it's time to move back home. With Linda in the USA and Jean in South Africa, I do feel responsible for our aging parents."

"Have you set a date for leaving?"

"Yes, I've booked a first-class ticket on a freighter ship that leaves mid-August."

"Sounds marvellous!" I replied, feeling slightly jealous but happy for Margaret.

There was such big hype over the Kirov Ballet coming to the O'Keefe Centre in June of 1974 that Margaret and I decided we would go. When we went down to the theatre to get tickets, they were selling out fast. We managed to get two in rear orchestra.

When we saw Peggy a few days later, we learned just how annoyed she was that we had failed to include her in our plans. "How could you think I wouldn't want to go?" she hurled at us, justifiably. Despite learning that it was a sold-out performance, Peggy was undaunted. She turned on her heel and walked away, saying, "I'll see you there. You'll see."

"What on earth do you think she means?" Margaret asked.

"How should I know? You know her as well as I do."

On the night of the performance, Peggy dressed in her little black dress and camel shawl. With her nicely-coiffed hair and well made-up face, she greeted us in the lobby with a big smile on her face, waving a ticket in her hand.

Confused at seeing her, I said, "I thought there were no more tickets!"

Her brown eyes twinkled and her sly smile gave it away—she had something up her sleeve. "With much pizzazz and gusto, I convinced them I was from the press."

"I suppose you batted those beautiful dark eyelashes at the fellow in the ticket wicket," Margaret said, laughing.

"I'll never tell," she said, waving her ticket in front orchestra at us as she ran off to her seat. "See you at intermission!"

Mikhail Baryshnikov, the lead Russian dancer, transformed himself across the stage in leaps and bounds. He moved with such grace, almost floating in mid-air. He was in a class of his own. We were totally mesmerized.

"Margaret," I said after we got into my car, "Baryshnikov danced so well, he may think we want to keep him!" We both giggled.

Arriving home, we turned on television to watch the news. We could not believe our eyes. On the television screen, we watched a clip of Baryshnikov being whisked away in a black car with the announcement, "He defected!"

"Wow. That's incredible!" I said.

"Fancy that!" Margaret replied in typical British fashion.

Margaret left as planned in August; Peggy and I missed her terribly. Fortunately, we had fond memories of the wonderful times we had together. Despite the distance between us, we managed to stay in touch. Peggy kept me informed about her son; I, on the other hand, remained in the dark about Robert. However, it became a lot easier for me to talk about my feelings with my parents, friends, and colleagues—but the yearning never went away.

MY TWO HUSBANDS

I will never forget the first time I met Leo. It was fall 1972. He was over six feet tall with wavy brown hair, a moustache and beard, and his sexy hazel eyes held me captive. That beautiful baritone voice with a mix of Australian, British and Canadian accents took my breath away. I knew he was taken, but we were both aware that we'd experienced an instant connection. An Australian by birth, Leo came to Canada in the 1950s to pursue a career in the film industry. His partner, Betty—a doctor at the hospital where I worked—was the one who introduced us. I was acutely aware that she was a very cloying partner.

Betty was a native Californian who hailed from Berkeley where she frequently returned for months at a time to check on her rental property. In 1975, while Betty was on an extended stay in California, Leo and I started dating, and it soon turned into a full-fledged affair.

Knowing that Leo had four children who lived with their mother in Montreal, I felt comfortable telling him about Robert.

"Have you tried to contact the doctor or the lawyer?" Leo asked me over cocktails at "The 22." Club 22 at the Windsor Arms hotel was a watering hole for celebrities, writers and many regulars.

"No," I replied, shaking my head, "I don't think they will share any information with me. It would give me such delight to know how he is doing. However, I need to remain realistic about my expectations."

After completing a certificate in Social Service Administration at Ryerson in 1974, I enrolled in a degree program in sociology at York University. Anxious to finish as quickly as possible, I took three courses a year. It was there that I met Kim, a single mother who was doing her psychology degree at York. Sometimes I baby-sat her daughter Jennifer. When I shared my story about Robert with Kim, she encouraged me to keep up the search.

"I've got an interview tomorrow with Metro Social Services, Homes for the Aged Division," I told Leo excitedly a week before Christmas. "It's for a position as Nurse Consultant." I got the job and started in January 1976.

That fall, I registered for *The Deviance of Sociology,* happy to have Judy Posner as a lecturer, having taken a previous course with her. Choosing a topic for a major paper on the subject, I decided to open up and tell my story. The title of the paper was "Being single and pregnant, circa 1962". In "An Afterwards", I wrote:

Writing this paper has given me new insight into myself as a person from a totally new perspective. Although I had been able to verbalize to others about my past stigma, I now am better able to see the process I went through in becoming stigmatized and how I attempted to hide from society. I can approach life more positively. Now I feel that I have the strength to face up to any of the past which may return to me. By that I mean I could honestly face my son and explain to him in a positive way that what I did 15 years ago was best for both of us.

"That was an excellent paper Jill. Very well constructed," Judy said handing it back to me. At last I felt it was acceptable to talk about giving up a son without feeling stigmatized.

I met Leo's children in 1978, and his eldest son (who was the same age as Robert) made me think more about my son. *By now he'd be sixteen. How is he doing in school? Does he ever ask about me?* I thought. I was comfortable sharing these thoughts with Leo.

When the Adoption Disclosure Registry became law in 1978, I was quick to send them all my pertinent information. However, it wasn't until March 1980 that I finally received a reply:

> Section 81 of the Child Welfare Act, 1978 provides an Adoption Disclosure Registry for adoptees who wish to establish contact with their birth parents, and for parents who wish to establish contact with their birth children. If both adoptee and a birth parent submit their names to the registry, this information can be exchanged. The adoptee, the adoptive parents, and the birth parent must give written permission to the disclosure.

Unless Robert also submitted a request to the Adoption Disclosure Registry, my hopes of us being united would be dashed.

Does he even know the Registry exists? I wondered.

By summer of 1978, I was promoted to the position of supervisor at the Geriatric Centre, an outpatient clinic for residents in all the Toronto Homes for the Aged. Sharing my story with my boss, she too encouraged me to try to locate Dr. Quigley.

An urgent visit to Dr. Papsin in June 1980 found me admitted to hospital for minor surgery. Reading a local newspaper, I spotted an advertisement for a nurse consultant with Sancella, a company that made disposable medical products. A few days later, the general and marketing managers put me through a rigorous interview that ended with, "Can you start on Monday?"

"No, not Monday but I can in two weeks," I happily responded.

When Leo and I were together it was electrifying. Just hearing his voice sent shivers up and down my spine. In winter of 1980, Leo invited me for drinks at Club 22.

"Jill, I've decided to move to Los Angeles. You know I want to be where the action is, and it's in Hollywood." Although disappointed, I was pleased for him when he landed a position as chief sound engineer with a small, independent company. Despite distance, our friendship never wavered.

"Let's go to the 22 after work on Friday," Pat suggested to Mary and me in March 1981. That evening I met Charles. He was a very, very funny man—bald lean, with beautiful clear blue eyes. His drawing card was his wicked sense of humour. Being from New Brunswick, he had a great gift of the gab and was quite the storyteller. People of all ages gravitated to him. I was one of them.

A manager at Bell Canada, Charles was divorced with two children, Lynne (age fifteen) and Jeff (age nine). They lived with their mother in the resort town of Barrie, Ontario. I knew our relationship was serious when he introduced me to his children in June. By August, he had moved into my house. Lynne, his daughter, moved in that fall to go to high school in Toronto.

"I hate being on the road so much," I lamented to Charles after being away nearly a week in November. "It feels I'm away more than I'm home."

"What would you like to do?"

I didn't even hesitate to answer, "I would love to start my own consulting company for seniors."

"That's a great idea," Charles responded. "I'll support you in setting it up and give you three to five years to make it viable."

Charles was a good business-minded person and liked what I was proposing. In November 1981, I registered Complete Geriatric Care and gave Sancella my resignation for the end of the year. I was now my own boss.

Charles and I took a trip to California in March 1982 to visit family and friends. We spent time with Betty in Berkeley and then with Leo in Los Angeles. Yes, they had separated. Although I was there with Charles, Leo's presence gave me a warm all-over feeling.

A few days after getting home, Charles snuggled up to me as I was preparing dinner.

"What are you doing December 18th?" His quirky smile and twinkle in his eyes gave me a strong hint that this was a proposal.

Wiping my hands on a paper towel, I laughed, saying, "Is that a proposal of marriage?"

"You bet it is. And your answer is?"

"Sounds good to me!"

We were married on December 18, 1982, at home with a handful of friends and relatives.

Once married, Charles was a candidate for an out-of-country transfer. Convinced it would be Saudi Arabia, Charles was surprised when he had a call from Dallas in June 1984.

"How would you like to work in Dallas with Northern Telecom?" they asked him.

Before we could set our sights on Dallas, Charles had another call:

"We need you to stop off and fix New York first."

As a result, we moved to New York City in September. Lynne found an apartment with a friend.

During those two years in New York City, it became brutally apparent that Charles was a full-blown alcoholic. Not only that—he was a pack-a-day smoker to boot. I should have left then, but I wasn't ready to throw in the towel. Being an optimistic person, I thought I could weather the storms and that everything would be okay. It wasn't. Al-Anon provided the support and guidance I needed to survive the onslaught of Charles' drinking bouts. I frequently called Leo in California for moral support. He always made me feel better.

When Charles wasn't drinking, he was charming, affable, interesting, engaging and genuinely delightful. Six months in New York was fantastic! One year was okay, but two years was too much. We moved back to Toronto in fall of 1986. That fall, Jeff moved in with us.

With every address change, I notified the Adoption Disclosure Registry, always optimistic my son would do the same. While in New York, I wrote to the Hamilton Children's Aid Society in 1985, hoping for updated information. This was their reply:

We have received your letter inquiring about Robert. As you know, he was placed privately, and we do not have a great deal of information about his adoptive parents. They were a couple in their mid-thirties, happily married, active in their church and community. The husband was a university graduate and had his own business. His wife was a high school graduate and had a supervisory position in an office. They had a daughter, also adopted. They were a capable, affectionate couple who enjoyed parenting, and Robert developed well. They were comfortable telling the children of their adoption.

We have had no contact with them since Robert's adoption was completed.

However, I already knew that information.

After a conversation with a colleague about my wish to find my son, I learned about Parent Finders. I joined in March 1987, but because their information was aimed at adoptees searching for biological parents, they were not helpful to me.

In 1987, Doug, a Nurse Associate of Complete Geriatric Care, secured us a contract at a retirement home in Hamilton.

Driving back and forth with Doug, I told him about Robert and my desire to know more about him. Quite moved, Doug piped up, "We need to find Dr. Quigley. Let's try getting an appointment with him."

"What would I have to lose?" I said. "Nothing else has worked."

Initially we learned Dr. Quigley had retired from practice. Undaunted, Doug persisted in his search. Dr. Quigley was doing a study at St. Joseph's Hospital in Uro-gynaecology.

Relating my story to Dr. Quigley, he said, "You should have contacted me ten years ago before I closed my practice. I don't have access to my files anymore."

I was thoroughly crushed! My hopes were completely dashed.

Doug would not give up. "Now we need to find Mr. White." He was the lawyer who handled the adoption.

Reaching his office receptionist, I was told, "We're sorry, but everything is on microfiche."

It was clear they were not interested in any further conversation. Basically, I was dismissed with, "These days, everything is stored off-site."

I should have been more persistent, demanding an appointment with one of the other lawyers. My two best resources were now dead ends.

Charles and I made frequent trips back to New York. Leafing through the airline magazine on one of those trips, my eyes almost popped out of my head. Staring back at me from the page was my old friend Bob being touted as an entrepreneur extraordinaire. The article done by a Globe and Mail journalist focussed on how he had more than once come back from the brink of bankruptcy. Back in Toronto, I contacted the journalist asking for the name and address of Bob's company. Nearly a decade had passed since seeing Bob. I wondered what response I would get when I called him.

"Bob here," I heard when he answered the phone.

"Hi Robert. Long time no see!"

"Jill!" he said. There was a long pause, then, "Jill. . .is that really you? How on earth did you find me?"

He roared with laughter when I told him about the article in the airline magazine, then said, "Let's have lunch!"

By then, Robert's four boys were young men, and he was still married. It was such fun catching up. For the next few years, we managed to find time for lunch or the occasional drink after work. He even came by our house and met Charles. However, by 1994, Bob and I had again drifted apart.

Charles and I had four different addresses after returning to Toronto. His drinking escalated to the point that, in 1991, I went home one day to see a bailiff's note on the door. Staring at the note, I couldn't believe my eyes. I was locked out of my own house. Charles had failed to pay the mortgage for over four months, forcing us to move into rental property for the next five years. In 1994, we declared bankruptcy. The shame of it has continued to haunt me. Again, I should have left then, but remained optimistic things would work out.

Always hopeful that one day my son and I would connect, I kept the Adoption Disclosure Registry up to date with name and address changes.

In August 1996, my father died. My mother sold the family home in King City and moved to a senior's apartment in

Toronto. With an inheritance from my father, I was able to purchase a bungalow in East York. By then things had started to really fall apart with Charles. In September he had triple bypass, and within three weeks of being discharged from hospital he was drinking and smoking again.

Before Charles' family arrived for Christmas that year, I said, "This is the very last Christmas we will be together. I want a divorce."

He was so drunk he didn't respond.

My colleagues knew how difficult life had become for me. By early January, one of my colleagues said, "Why don't you take some time off to think about what you want to do?"

"Yes, you're right," I said. "It's a great idea. I do need to think things through."

Immediately I called Leo to discuss my options.

"Why don't you come to LA for a visit?" he said.

That voice! That marvellous voice turned me into a blithering idiot. I was so excited at the prospect of seeing Leo again I could hardly contain my composure. I felt like a teenager being asked out on a first date.

"How can I turn down such a proposal?" I said. "I would love to see you in LA."

"Great—when can I expect you?"

It was like falling in love all over again. I went for a week in January 1997 and stayed ten days. I was totally swept off my feet. Palpitations, blushing, being giddy—all the signs of being in love leapt to the forefront. Life was marvellous!

Returning to Toronto was a real downer. Charles knew our marriage was over, but he was still there. We separated shortly after my trip to California and were divorced in 1999.

From 1997 – 2003, Leo and I kept Air Canada in business by flying back and forth. Christmas of 1999 I waited for Leo at Pearson airport along with several other impatient people. The plane was late. One lady who was pacing back and forth kept looking at her watch and then at the arrivals board. I said to her, "You must be waiting for someone on the LA flight."

"Yes, my daughter who lives in Manhattan Beach is coming home for Christmas." We continued to chat and I eventually learned she was a financial planner.

"Why don't we exchange business cards? I am an elder-care consultant."

When she handed me her business card, I stood transfixed, staring at her card. I felt a lump in my throat, and my heart began to pound. It read Mary Henderson. Gaining my composure, I said, "When I was a teenager, my friend Bob Baxter had a good friend named George Henderson whom he used to bring to my house."

Before I could say another word, she said, "George is my husband!"

In a very excited voice, I asked, "Do you ever see Bob now?"

With careful deliberation, Mary replied, "We heard Bob had passed away."

No! Not Bob! Tears filled my eyes as I realized I would never again see that charming fellow who stole my heart as a teenager. He would have been only in his fifties. I pulled a tissue out of my purse and wiped my eyes, thanking her for this information.

On June 15th 2002, I married the love of my life. Upon returning from our honeymoon, I sent another letter off to the Adoption Disclosure Registry, always hopeful Robert would do the same.

THE END OF THE LINE

"Your mother is not responding," came the call from the nursing home. "What do you mean, not responding?" I anxiously asked. I felt a knot forming in my stomach.

"After breakfast your mother had a spell, so we put her back to bed."

What the nurse was saying didn't make sense. "What kind of a spell did she have?"

"Well, to be honest, we haven't been able to rouse her since then."

My mind became a blur. With a pounding heart and tightness in my chest, tears welled up in my eyes before rolling slowly down my cheeks. What could possibly have happened? Glancing at my watch, I noted it was almost noon.

"I will be there shortly," I said choking back the tears. I immediately called Leo at home to tell him what I knew. I told him that I would pick him up before going to the nursing home.

Closing down my computer and collecting my belongings, I told my colleagues what I knew and that I would be leaving immediately.

On the way home, I began to reflect on my mother's life as I knew it. I had a gut feeling that she had likely suffered a stroke. Over and over I kept thinking about her last words the day before when I left her room. Just as I'd reached the hall, I'd heard, "Jill. . .Jill!"

Turning around, I hurried back to her room. "What is it, Mother?"

Holding up the empty cookie tin, she asked, "Can you bring me some arrowroot cookies when you come in tomorrow?"

"Of course I will," I said with enthusiasm. "See you then."

It was Friday June 6, 2009. Mother would turn ninety-seven on August 7th. Despite her many physical frailties, she maintained an optimistic outlook on life. An avid baseball fan, she loved watching the Blue Jays on television. Being mentally alert at her age is something we all hoped to achieve. Everyone always commented on her indomitable spirit. She was the last of six, having outlived her baby sister by well over a decade. Mother had no formal education beyond grade nine. At the age of fourteen, she was forced to go out to work as a domestic. Her only brother was married to my dad's only sister. It was during a visit to them in 1933 that she met my dad. They were married in 1936. I was the firstborn child, arriving in winter of 1940. A second daughter, born in summer of 1941, only lived five days, making me an only child. Like every other marriage, theirs had its ups and downs. Despite the difficulties, they weathered the storms with aplomb. Mother had a real zest for life.

However, on April 24th, the day she went into the nursing home, she said, "I really don't want to be in this world anymore." Mother had always hoped to pass away sitting in her chair watching her beloved Blue Jays on television.

"Honey, I am so glad the nurses had the respect to pull the curtain around mom's bed," I said as Leo and I entered her room. Thankfully, her roommate was nowhere to be seen. Peering around the curtain, I was happy to see Mother dressed in navy slacks and a matching floral blouse with the string of pearls around her neck—and of course, she had on the matching earrings.

Despite her elder years, she always wanted to look her best. "Is my hair okay?" she would ask, patting the top of her head. "Are you sure it's not sticking up in the back?" She really didn't look or act like an old person.

I stood there watching and listening to her much-laboured breathing. Turning to Leo, I said, "Mother has definitely had a stroke." My heart ached with the realization that my mother was dying. I pulled out a tissue from my purse to wipe the tears that were running down my cheeks. When I gained composure, Leo and I went to talk to the nurses.

"Would you like us to send her to hospital?" The head nurse asked.

I recalled when my dad had a stroke in 1996, and how Mother called 911. After they performed CPR, he was resuscitated but was unconscious; he was sent to the hospital where he died a day and a half later.

"If that happens to me, please don't call the ambulance," were her words to me.

"No, please just keep her comfortable," I said to the nurse. "And please keep me posted on any changes. Leo and I will be at home."

It was just after four o'clock when the phone rang. That achy feeling washed over me like I had the flu. Despite being somewhat prepared, I knew the news wasn't going to be good.

"Jill," said the head nurse in a quiet voice, "Your mother passed away a few minutes ago."

I thanked her, hung up the phone, then burst into tears. My once robust, active, involved, wonderful, loving, and caring mother was gone.

Leo held out his hand as I put down the receiver. I sat down beside him on the sofa and whispered, "Mother passed away just after four o'clock." Then I murmured, to no one in particular, "Thank you, God—her suffering was short. Now I really am an orphan—the end of the line." While I was still holding Leo's hand, an optimistic part of me said, *Maybe I will find my son, and then I won't be the end of the line after all.*

A FINAL PLEA

After placing mother's ashes in the ground the end of June, I remembered the Adoption Registry had officially opened June 1st. *Now I can begin my search for Robert,* I thought. *Even if I find him, it makes me sad knowing my mother will not share that happiness with me.*

The original opening of the Adoption Registry was to be January 2008. In December 2007, lawyer Clayton Ruby filed a Class Action suit against the Government. A number of adoptees and birth mothers did not want disclosure. The passing of the bill was delayed another eighteen months. I felt like a dark black cloud loomed overhead. Waiting those eighteen months was an eternity. *What if Robert has decided he doesn't want contact with me?* I thought. *I must not keep my hopes up too high.*

Finally the time arrived to make my request. With a twinge of hope on June 25th, I submitted my request to the Attorney General's office for the original and adopted birth certificates for Robert. Knowing how slowly the wheels of Government churned, I didn't expect a reply anytime soon.

A few days later, I wrote a letter of appreciation to NDP MPP Marilyn Churley. I wanted to thank her for her tenacity in the introduction of a private member's Bill to open the

Adoption Disclosure Registry. All I could do now was cross my fingers and wait.

AN EPIC MEETING

Stepping out of the shower, I dried myself and carefully laid my makeup on the bathroom counter. Next, I sprayed my trademark "Je Reviens" behind my ears, the crooks of my arms, and on the front of my neck. Normally I didn't bother with a foundation, but that night I did. I wanted everything to be perfect. Looking into the mirror, I was pleased the way I had applied my make-up. After stepping into my black slacks, I pulled the purple blouse over my head then put my feet into black leather pumps, deliberating about what jewellery to add. I decided on the pearls and matching earrings Leo gave me one Christmas. My purple blazer topped off the outfit. The last thing I did was put my iris pin on the left lapel.

Into my big leather bag I placed photographs of my parents and me, copies of the two birth certificates Andrew asked me to bring along, the paper I did on being stigmatized, the book I had written, and of course, a box of facial tissue in case I had a crying jag. *How will I actually feel when Andrew and I meet face to face?* I wondered. *This is a journey I have endured for many years. Maybe now I will reach my destination.*

Immediately my mind drifted back to arriving home after a conference on December 4th, 2009.

"There's a letter for you from the Attorney General's Office," Leo announced. Then, in an accusatory tone he said, "What have you done?"

I burst into laughter as I took the envelope from him, because I knew the contents.

I gently pulled everything out of the envelope being, very careful not to tear anything inside. Wanting to view the legal-sized forms, I merely glanced at the cover letter. The first document was a copy of the original birth certificate with the name Robert that I had given him. The other document was a copy of the adoption birth certificate with names of the key players blackened out. Laughing and crying at the same time while jumping up and down, I excitedly said to Leo, "My son's name is Andrew Dunbar Pringle!"

"Let's Google him," Leo suggested.

When I Googled Andrew Dunbar Pringle, a page popped up with pictures of him and his two partners. "My son is a lawyer in Ancaster," I said with delight. Ancaster is a small town near Hamilton where he was born. Wanting to read everything, I kept scrolling down the page to learn he had a wife and two children—my grandchildren!

When I clicked on his photo, Leo exclaimed, "He looks exactly like your father!"

That he did indeed. The family resemblance was overwhelming. It was hard not to take my eyes off Andrew. There was no doubt in my mind that this person was indeed my son.

"Honey, the butterflies in my stomach are trying to escape," I said. "I can hear my heart pounding. I feel light-headed.

After all this time, I finally have the information. What's my next step?"

"Let's not rush into things," Leo suggested.

Before the Adoption Disclosure Registry was opened, great care would have been taken before our initial meeting. A counsellor would have worked with both of us to smooth the way for our meeting. Things were different now. I knew who he was and where he practised law.

"Why don't you call Barbro to discuss it with her first?" Leo suggested. Barbro was my friend and lawyer.

As soon as I heard her voice, I blurted out, "Barbro, I've found my son, and he is a lawyer in Ancaster!"

"Well, that really is good news," she replied, knowing how hard I had searched over the years.

"It sure is. The only listing for him is his office and nothing for his home."

"How be I do a search for you and get back to you once I have the information?" she said.

"That would be great!" I responded. "Thanks!"

While waiting for that phone call, my nerves were shot. Knowing my anxiety level was high, Leo tried to calm me down.

"Barbro has to fit your request into her regular working day so, be patient," he said.

Barbro called the next day. "Your son lives in Ancaster, and the house is registered in his wife's name," she said.

Hearing Barbro say *your son* turned me into a blithering idiot.

Gaining composure, I asked, "What is his home number?"

After thanking her, Leo and I sat down to map out a plan on how best to make contact. I was no shrinking violet, so I was most anxious to get on with the task at hand.

"Wynne, Dingwall and Pringle," said the receptionist when I called Andrew at work the next day.

"Do you have an Andrew Dunbar Pringle working there?" I enquired.

"No, I'm sorry," she replied and hung up. Certain that I had the correct number, I was totally perplexed by this response. From the look on Leo's face, I knew he was wondering what had happened.

"They said there was no Andrew Dunbar Pringle there. I know it was the right number," I said.

Not easily put off, I called twice the next day and received the same response. This had me totally befuddled. The palpitations in my chest were so strong I felt I was going to explode. I had a real ache in my heart. I couldn't stop thinking about him.

With sweaty palms, butterflies in my stomach, and my heart pounding, I called his home telephone number. It was 6:30 in the evening. A young boy answered and said, "Hello?"

Oh my God, this must be my grandson, I thought. With weak knees, I swallowed to moisten my dry throat,

"Could I speak to Andrew Dunbar Pringle?"

"My dad won't be home until after eight o'clock," came the response.

"Thank you!" I said, and hung up. Looking at Leo with a wide grin, I said, "Oh my goodness, I think I just spoke to my grandson. His dad won't be home until eight o'clock."

Knowing my angst at more waiting, Leo gently hugged me, saying, "You will just have to call him later."

Watching the clock ticking away was like watching paint dry on a wall. I kept running back to the computer to stare at his picture. I was covered in goosebumps, and tingly feelings welled up inside of me. Tears would start filling my eyes, then I would burst out laughing. I decided to wait an extra half-hour before calling back.

"Hello?" came from the same young voice from my first telephone call.

"Could I speak to Andrew Dunbar Pringle?"

"Just a minute," he answered. I heard him yell, "Dad, it's for you!"

I heard shuffling before I heard his voice. "Hello?"

"Are you Andrew Dunbar Pringle?" I asked very nervously.

"Yes," he answered.

Oh, my God, I am really talking to the son I gave up forty-seven years ago. Get yourself together.

"Are you sitting down?"

"Should I be?"

"You might want to," I replied.

"Just a minute," he said, right before hearing him running up a flight of stairs.

"You can hang up now," I heard him say to his son. Now it was my turn.

Gathering all my courage while trying to remain calm, I said, "Andrew, my name is Jill O'Donnell. I have two pieces of paper in my hand that give me reason to believe I am your biological mother."

There was only a very short pause before he said, "Really?" It was said with a warm exclamation. "How did you find me?"

I explained about the opening of the Adoption Registry. Andrew always knew he was adopted, and although surprised at my sudden appearance in his life, it was not unexpected. We talked incessantly for over an hour, questioning each other back and forth, trying to fill in forty-seven years. There were no pauses in our conversation. It just flowed easily as we learned more about each other, trying to decide on a time and place to meet.

"Andrew, my husband Leo and I are going to London, England for twelve days over Christmas. However, now that I've made contact with you, it would be wonderful if we could meet before we go away."

"When will you be away?"

"We leave December 23rd and will not be home until January 1st.

"Let me check my calendar and I'll get back to you. What is your home telephone number?"

After putting my mother's ashes into the grave with my father in July, we had arranged to go to London over Christmas. As an only child I was always there for Mother. Her passing was a gift of freedom to go away at Christmas. Desperate to see Andrew, I hoped against all hope he could fit me into his schedule.

Arriving home around six o'clock Friday night, a smiling Leo said, "Andrew called and wants you to call him back."

"Did you talk to him?"

"Yes, we talked for about a half hour

"What did you talk about?"

"He wanted to know how long you had been searching for him and how long had I known about him." Leo told Andrew he had met me in 1972 and knew shortly after we met that I had wanted to find him.

Andrew's immediate response was, "So she has been looking for me for a very long time."

It took me just seconds to dial his home number. It was wonderful to hear that Andrew had such a lengthy conversation with Leo.

"My practice is so busy this time of year. Do you mind if we put our meeting off until the New Year?"

"I understand," I said, trying to keep the disappointment out of my voice. "We can set something up when I get back."

Upon our return from the UK, I was quite bowled over to find an email from Andrew. Again, tears welled up in my eyes as I read the email.

> Jill:
>
> Welcome back from London.
>
> I too look forward to meeting you. I agree with you—it will be an emotional event. Over the years, I often wondered who you were and where you were. I now know the answers to those questions. Somehow, I had envisioned you still being in the Hamilton area. I was therefore surprised to hear that your time in Hamilton was actually quite brief. Except for going away to university, I have spent my life in this area. The bigger surprise was finding out that I had, albeit for a very brief period of time, another name. I confess that has created an odd feeling in me.

In terms of how we go about organizing a time and place to meet, since you've started by e-mail, let's continue it that way. If possible, I'd like to set this up during the week. We ski in Ellicottville, New York (about 2 hours from here) and are away most winter weekends. I'd also prefer to come to Toronto to see you. What would you think of meeting late afternoon/early evening in Toronto some time in the coming weeks?

By the way, congratulations on your sleuthing work in finding me. It sounds like it took quite a bit of your time and energy over the years. Even with that, it took some legislative changes to finally help bring your search to a conclusion. You made it a memorable Christmas for me.

Andrew

DINING WITH ANDREW

"May I take your coat?" The maître d' at the Epic restaurant asked, smiling warmly. Since making contact with Andrew in early December I had been on cloud nine. I hadn't been able to stop thinking about him. Finally, the day had arrived. I was led to a quiet area at the back of the dining room.

A gentleman rose as we approached. I felt the hair on the back of my neck stand straight up. *He looks exactly like my dad*, I thought. He was of medium build with a square jaw, high forehead, broad nose, and his ears were close to his head. I could hear my heart pounding. Staying calm, cool, and collected wasn't easy. I felt like a kid in a candy store. This was the most significant meeting of my life.

It was like looking into a mirror, except I was looking into the eyes of a grown man. The only difference was that he had a bald head. He had a broad, happy smile as he came towards me from the back of the table.

"Hi Jill, it's great to finally meet you," he said.

"Hello, Andrew," I said with such joy in my heart. "I too am delighted to finally meet you!" We hugged and kissed like it was the most natural thing for a mother and son to do.

"Can I offer you a drink?" the waiter asked as he handed us our menus.

"A white wine spritzer please," I responded, glancing over at Andrew who had a cocktail in front of him.

"I hope you don't mind. I ordered a drink to calm my nerves," he said. We laughed as we clinked glasses to honour this epic occasion. Immediately we launched into conversation, bantering back and forth about our lives over the previous forty-seven years.

"Would you like to order now?" The waiter had returned ready to take our order. The menus in front of us were still unopened.

"Thank you, but please give us some more time," I requested. Andrew laughed when I pulled out the box of facial tissues. "Hopefully I will be able to contain my joy without resorting to tears," I said.

What was so amazing is that not only did we look alike—the clothes we wore were a similar shade of purple. There was no doubt in my mind that Andrew was my son.

"Was John bald?" Andrew asked, rubbing his hand over his head. I had previously told him his biological father's name was John.

"No, Andrew, baldness is passed on by the mother. Actually, my father was almost bald." I noticed that Andrew actually chose to shave his head completely. Sharing photos of childhood and family stories filled every minute. There were no gaps in our conversation.

"How are your adoptive parents? They must be very special!"

"My adoptive mother died of an aneurysm when she was just sixty-one years old, the week before Sandi and I were married in 1991. My father remarried ten years ago."

"I am so sorry to hear about your adopted mother," I said.

Looking me straight in the eye, Andrew said, "You are the only mother I have now. I cannot call you Mother yet, but I might in the future." Just hearing him say that made my eyes moisten. I didn't care what he called me as long as we could be together. He said he had no trouble with me calling him my son, but it is was his adoptive parents who raised him, and they would always be Mom and Dad to him.

"I understand you wanted me to learn to play the piano," Andrew commented.

"Well, both John and I played the piano, and John also played the flute and clarinet. He was quite talented musically. Did you learn to play the piano?"

'Yes, but I gave it up after high school. I can still play, though."

Hearing all the wonderful things he did while growing up gave me reason to believe they must have been terrific parents—another indication that I'd made the right decision at the time.

"Now, tell me about your wife and children."

I was thrilled to bits hearing about his wife, Sandi, and his two children, Victoria (sixteen) and Robert (twelve). How strange—I'd named him Robert, and now he had named his own son Robert, having no idea of his previous name.

During our time together, we shared so many stories that linked our lives together. I told him about the time in 2005 when Leo and I were in London, England, staying with my old roommate, Margaret, who had a New Age shop, The Eclipse. Margaret invited me to have a tarot card reading by Phillipa.

As soon as I sat down opposite Phillipa, she began laying out the tarot cards. "You will be seeing your son soon," was the first thing she'd said. I felt the blood drain out of my face. "Is something wrong?" she'd asked, looking a bit perplexed.

Shaking my head, I replied, "No, I will tell you after you finish my reading *Is what I am hearing really possible?* She went on to say my grandson and granddaughter would be with my son. The reading was beginning to freak me right out. I felt a tightening in my chest just listening to her. *Could it be true—I have a grandson and granddaughter?*

When it was over, I told Philippa my story. She sounded so confident, saying, "You will see him soon."

Aside from me naming him Robert and him naming his son Robert, we discovered that Andrew and I were both York University Alumni. He did his under-graduate commerce degree at Queen's University in Kingston but did his law degree at Osgoode Law School at York University. He was called to the bar on my fifty-third birthday, February 9, 1993. He too had made attempts to speak to Mr. White. Apparently, Mr. White, the lawyer, had become a judge around the time Andrew was articling, and had been dismissive when Andrew enquired about finding me. Strangely enough, we also like the same authors.

Our time together absolutely flew by. In order for Andrew to catch the last train to Burlington, we had to call it a night.

"Do you have any other children?" Andrew asked as we stood up to leave. I knew he had an adopted sister, but I learned his adoptive parents had a son three years younger than Andrew.

"No, you are my only child," I said.

He looked at me in surprise. "Please understand, I need time to tell my kids, my sister Jane, my brother Jake, and my father that we have met. Sandi knows already," he said.

How exciting! I thought. *He wants me to meet his wife and children. Obviously Andrew is prepared for me to be a part of his life.*

"I do understand, and will leave it up to you to decide our next meeting."

Handing me my coat, the maître d' again smiled warmly and asked," How was your meeting?"

Her comment startled me, but before I could say anything, Andrew piped up. "I told her about our meeting when I arrived in case we got carried away with emotion. Obviously there was nothing to worry about."

As I put my arms into the sleeves of my coat, I smiled. "It was the very best ever," I said, "thank you."

Standing in the lobby of the Royal York, I shed tears of joy. We hugged and kissed and hugged again. Andrew headed to Union Station, and I headed to the parking garage. It was indeed an epic occasion!

NOT THE LAST CHAPTER

On February 9, 2010, I answered a knock at the door. A delivery man asked, "Are you Jill O'Donnell?" As I nodded, he thrust a long grey box into my arms then sped away. A most elegant selection of cut spring flowers with birthday wishes from Andrew brought tears of happiness. This was my very first gift from my son!

On Mother's Day, I received more flowers and a very touching card signed "From your son." Again, I was bowled over at such a show of affection from Andrew.

We continued to share regular emails and got to know more about each other. In July, Andrew emailed an invitation for Leo and me to join him and his wife Sandi at the Old Mill Restaurant in Ancaster for brunch.

It was a lovely warm summer day for the drive to Ancaster. The bright blue sky was dotted with fluffy white clouds. As we emerged from our car, a sweet scent of flowers filled the air around us. Looking ahead, we could see the Old Mill. There was a beautiful cascading waterfall beside us as we descended the steps to the restaurant, and it was a perfect backdrop to the Mill. Everywhere cameras clicked as people filed in front of the falls to have their photos taken.

"Welcome," Andrew said as he greeted us in the main doorway, giving me a hug and a kiss. "We watched you come down the stairs."

"Hi Andrew, this is Leo," I said. The two men shook hands. Andrew led us to a table overlooking the falls. A pretty, petite lady with shoulder-length straight blonde hair and smiling brown eyes stood up. "Jill, Leo, this is my wife, Sandi."

Sandi was warm and inviting. I immediately felt comfortable in her presence. "I'm so happy to meet you," I said, leaning towards her.

"Me too," she replied as we hugged and kissed. Then spontaneously, Sandi hugged Leo. "Jill, Andrew has told me so much about you. Now I'm looking forward to getting to know you, too."

Conversation flowed easily as we enjoyed the magnificent and tasty display of food. Learning Sandi was Italian, I immediately enquired, "Do your children speak Italian?"

"Well, my mother looked after Victoria growing up, so yes, she speaks pretty good Italian. However, Robert doesn't," she said. Sandi told us she was an education assistant at a local high school working with physically and mentally challenged youth. *She must have the patience of a saint,* I thought when she described some of her students.

I learned that Andrew's law practice was devoted mainly to business law, real estate, Wills, and Powers of Attorney. "The location of my office allows me to go home for lunch," he informed us, smiling.

What a joyful occasion it was spending our mid-day Sunday with Andrew and Sandi.

"Are you in a hurry to get home?" Andrew asked as we got up from the table. "I would really like to see where you lived in Hamilton, if you have the time to show me. We can leave your car here and go in mine. Sandi has an errand to run, so she brought her own car." It was a simple request and one I was happy to share with Andrew. When we found the house, Andrew exclaimed, "It sure is close to the hospital. Both Victoria and Robert were born at St. Joseph's hospital. And so were Sandi and my adopted sister, Jane." I knew he was pleased that we took the time to see where I lived in Hamilton.

Of course, I was truly ecstatic when, in September, Andrew informed me that he had told his children about me. "I never said this before, but Victoria actually asked me if I knew about my medical background before you and I met. I have now told her about meeting you. She thinks that's terrific." We set Sunday, October 17th 2010 for dinner at our place.

Despite the fact that we were strangers meeting for the first time, Victoria and Robert greeted us exactly the same way their parents did—with hugs and kisses. Robert, a rather shy, retiring, and very nice looking teen-ager, remained quiet, but responded when spoken to. Victoria was pretty, was more outgoing, and joined in conversation readily. They were terrific teenagers— well-behaved, warm, and engaging. It was a clear that Andrew and Sandi were wonderful parents.

Cleaning up after they left, I had an epiphany. "Leo, today was Sandi's birthday. She gave up her day for me to meet my grandchildren."

"I'd say that's a pretty nice daughter-in-law you have there," Leo responded.

For many years, I have always put out a Christmas newsletter covering key events that have gone on during the year. Telling this to Andrew while at his home in early December 2010, Sandi laughed and piped up, "Andrew does a Christmas letter, too." Then she added, "The more you two are together, the more alike you are." Andrew and I both laughed at her observation. We'd already figured that out.

Our relationship continues to grow and thrive. I am blessed it has turned out so well. My granddaughter Victoria graduated as a Registered Practical Nurse in 2014. Robert will be entering his last year of high school in the fall.

Sharing my story with family, friends and colleagues, I always get the same feedback: "What an incredible story. You are so lucky." That I am!

Not too long after Andrew and I met, I sent another letter off to Marilyn Churley, NDP MPP, thanking her for introducing her private member's bill to open the Adoption Registry. This time I told her I had found my son and how our relationship has changed my life forever. I am saddened that my mother did not get to meet Andrew, the grandson she always hoped to know. With her passing in 2009, I thought I was the end of the line. When I told Andrew, he was quick to reply,

"Not so—now there are two generations coming after you."

In many ways, I have reached my destination, but the real journey is just beginning.

CPSIA information can be obtained at www.ICGtesting.com
Printed in the USA
LVOW10*0155101014

408103LV00002B/7/P